Feel The Rain

Lisa Bain

Feel The Rain

Stories from a Decade of Divine Detours
and Dancing in the Storms

By Lisa Bain

STORIA PUBLISHING

TULSA, OKLAHOMA
STORIAWRITER.COM

All Scripture quotations, unless otherwise indicated, are taken from The Holy Bible, New International Version ® , NIV ®. Copyright © 1973, 1978, 1984, 2011 by Biblica, Inc. ™ Used by permission of Zondervan. All rights reserved worldwide. www.zondervan.com. The "NIV" and "New International Version" are trademarks registered in the United States Paten and Trademark Office by Biblica, Inc. ™

Book design by Megan Morrow

ISBN 979-8-9857364-3-4

Printed in the United States of America

Storia Editing and Publishing, LLC

storiawriter.com

Table of Contents

This book is dedicated to my wonderful husband, Skipper Bain. When I was tempted to put the pen down, he encouraged me to keep going. I am thankful God's divine detours led me straight to him.

Foreword

As Co-Founder and Executive Director of the Little Light House, a Christian Developmental Center for children with special needs, I never tired of witnessing the blessings God bestowed on our precious students and their families. As a faith ministry reliant on donations for our support, we were amazed at the outpouring of love from the community. It seemed there was always something wonderful happening. Sometimes it was the donation of a new piece of equipment. Other days, it might be a friend stopping by to contribute financially or drop off needed supplies. But one particular day, I learned we were expecting two special guests. A lovely lady named Lisa Bain was coming by, with the one and only Mavis Pearl, an English bulldog known for her gentle manner, her broad smile, and the brightly colored tutus she wore! Lisa and Mavis would walk from classroom to classroom, allowing the children to lavish their love on Mavis. And Mavis loved them right back. To make it even more special, the two always came bearing gifts for every child. We looked forward to their visits and the joy and laughter they brought. I understood the children's fascination and at-tachment to the twosome because Lisa brightened every room she entered. The children were drawn to her beautiful spirit, her kindness, generosity, love, and the pure joy she created.

It seemed this remarkable lady's life mission was to minister hope, happiness, and love to a hurting world. After that first meeting, I knew she was fulfilling her mission.

Over the years, I've had the privilege of getting to know Lisa, and I consider her one of my most treasured friends. After a recent cancer diagnosis, I was overwhelmed by her compassion and the love she poured out to me and my family during my illness. I am consistently fascinated by her boundless energy, her zeal for life, and her inexhaustible supply of compassion and unconditional love for others!

In witnessing the amazing way Lisa brings so much light to her world, there might be some who are curious to know the source of her strength. I have good news! You will find the answer to that question within these pages.

Feel the Rain allows the reader a peek into the transparent heart, soul, and life of Lisa Bain. Like all of us, Lisa has experienced the exhilarating joy of life's mountaintop moments. She has also endured the devastation and loneliness of deep valleys where disappointment, loss and betrayal live. This book reminds us that our precious Lord and Savior doesn't want us to walk through those valleys alone. He wants to be with us every step of the way. His heart's desire is to encourage us, give us all the strength we need and guide us to perfect victory. Through Lisa's willingness to be real with her world, we witness the faithfulness of God when a soul is yielded to Him.

Whether you read *Feel the Rain* as a devotional for daily inspiration, or from cover-to-cover to gain insights for your personal spiritual growth, you will not be disappointed. Instead, your heart will be lifted and, if you are like me, encouraged towards a closer, deeper, and more intimate walk with our Lord and Savior, Jesus Christ.

I'm grateful to Lisa for her willingness to share these priceless life lessons. As you read this book, you will draw closer to the heart of God and experience the richness of His love and grace.

Trust in the Lord with all your heart and lean not on your own understanding. (Proverbs 3:5)

Marcia Mitchell
Co-Founder and Former CEO
Little Light House, Inc.

Introduction

Before we start, you should know that sometimes I love rain. The fresh smell of a spring downpour makes my senses come alive, and I have this strange desire to take my shoes off and stomp through puddles. As a little girl, I couldn't resist a fresh rain puddle. One stomp, and the frilly dress Mom had put me in was a mess of brown splotches and rings.

But other times, I shake my fist at the rain. It messes up my running schedule and forces me to cancel outdoor plans. It also makes my dogs pout when they can't take their usual morning walk. I also love a good surprise but hate unexpected interruptions. And a detour when I'm in a hurry makes me crazy. Life is made up of these highs and lows, storms and sunshine.

I started writing on my blog in 2010, after Mom was diagnosed with cancer and I got a surprise diagnosis of a cocktail of autoimmune diseases, most of which I couldn't even pronounce. It felt like a huge rainstorm that wouldn't stop, but at its beginning, Mom had encouraged me to write. I protested to her that I'm not a writer, but that didn't matter. We were starting a journey, and writing would help me put things in perspective and sort out the craziness. Mom also added that my writing could benefit others who were walking a similar path. That made sense, so I began a blog and have continued posting on it for over a decade.

But this book is not only for those who are facing cancer, illness, or other crisis situations. It's for anyone who has walked through the day wondering if God has forgotten them or questioning whether they have a purpose. Does God really speak to us in the mundane moments of life? Are we really safe in His hands? And if we're stuck in a downpour, should we stomp in the puddles or run for shelter?

This book is a compilation of posts from my blog and new writings you won't find anywhere else. Think of it as a love letter to remind you that storms will come and rain will fall, but God is in every drop, waiting for us to discover joy and see the miracles.

So, set your umbrella aside and follow me out into the downpour!

Lisa Bain
June 15, 2022

Faith Walking

This is My Story, and My Song

I can still remember the smell of sweet cinnamon and polished wood in the sanctuary as we sat each week on cushioned pews. On Sunday mornings, Miss Bertha sat in the front, and I can still hear her rambunctious "amens." Our voices blended as we sang the hymns each week, but my mind was not on the music. I wanted that hour to pass faster so we could get to my favorite after-church restaurant, Casa Bonita. There was one hymn, *Blessed Assurance*, that always held my attention, because it was about stories.

This is my story, this is my song. Praising my Savior all the day long. It felt like a song just for me. Each time we sang this hymn, I pictured myself reading a storybook aloud. It was my story, and I could sing it!

I changed my iTunes list so I could listen to the old hymns on my prayer walks. I've had Jadon Lavik's hymn album, *Roots Run Deep*, on repeat, loving and savoring every note and each comforting word. Music is an important part of my life. My mom was a piano teacher, and I grew up singing. I quit piano because I never liked to practice, but thanks to Mom, I inherited a love for music that went beyond repeating scales and learning theory. God changes me through the words and notes of melodies and lyrics.

During this past season of pandemic, I've been listening to music non-stop, and on my prayer walk, one song caused me to slow down and turn up the volume. As I listened to it, I was back in that cushioned pew singing with Mom and Dad, surrounded by others who were proclaiming, *This is my story, this is my song. Praising my Savior all the day long!* Through the years, I have learned to be thankful for my story, even though it contains dark storms as well as bright sunshine. God has given each of us a story and a song that belongs only to us. Our story is born and blessed by Him, and even the broken ones may help change or save someone's life. But the stories need to be shared.

In a crowded meeting, I listened to a woman share her story of hope and redemption. I was amazed by what she walked through and how she had emerged victorious. "You need to share this with others," I told her. She responded she had never thought about it and wondered who would want to hear it. So many times, we think our stories won't be moving or dramatic enough, but someone who is walking the same journey needs your voice. They need your story.

Fannie Crosby, who wrote *Blessed Assurance*, experienced blindness, widowhood, deaths of family members, and continuous obstacles. In 1873, during one of the most painful moments in her life, she wrote this song. She embraced her story and walked with praise and anticipation of "a foretaste of glory divine." Jesus was her story! Reading about Fannie made the song, and the memories, even more special.

The older I get, the more I learn to embrace every moment of my story. Both storms and sunshine have brought me to a place of knowing that my story is blessed, and that Jesus is mine. He is the Author who weaves our stories into a beautiful tapestry that doesn't hide the dark places. There are seasons of rest in our stories as we watch and wait for the calm after the storm. When it comes, we continue walking with peace and blessed assurance.

Think of everything you have endured and all that you have overcome. Listen to *Blessed Assurance* and meditate on the words. This is your story. This is your song. And you are blessed all day long. Maybe the valley is dark, and the pieces of your life are scattered at your feet. It's a chapter in your story – a verse in your song. Sing it loud, and with feeling. And someday, you will share it with someone who needs to know they aren't alone.

Pruning

Mom had a green thumb and so does my sister. Me? Not so much. If a cactus survives in my house for a week, I get excited. As a child, I watched Mom plant flowers and work her garden in a way that seemed effortless. She knew what to do and, like a talented gardener, when to do it. I have a vivid childhood memory of our front flower bed filled with beautiful, fragrant rose bushes. But in early winter, Mom would trim those bushes until they were nothing but sticks.

"Mom, what are you doing?" I asked her once. "Now they're just ugly and bare!"

As we sat on the porch swing together, she explained to me that those rose bushes were only beautiful because of the cutting. The pruning. And for four or five months, our front flower bed was nothing but pathetic sticks in the ground. But when spring came, hundreds of tiny buds grew on the sticks, and then, one by one, those buds opened into vibrant colors. The sticks transformed into abundant, breathtaking roses that delighted our neighbors.

Years later, during one of her chemo treatments, Mom and I talked about dreams. I always shared with her every detail of my deepest dreams, and she held them close to her heart.

She told me God wants us to dream big. He puts them in our hearts for His purposes, but He doesn't want us to exclude Him while we are chasing them.

The dreams God planted in my heart have required pruning, a cutting away of all that was unnecessary. Those are the broken places. And sometimes He cuts away people from our lives who don't fit into the dream or destiny He has for us. It is painful at the time, but He is protecting the dream from anything that would hinder its growth. He wants our dreams to bring forth good fruit.

These last few years, it has felt like my dreams have been laid down, and at times, like they were dying. I was in the winter season, feeling like those pathetic sticks of rose bushes. It was cold, lonely, and every part of me felt bare, vulnerable, and stuck. Later, what I realized is that the greatest breakthrough toward realizing my dream came after a time of pruning and then surrender. I had to ask questions like, "Was this my dream, or His?" It's amazing how authentic answers come to light during the pruning. Things are cleaned and cleansed, and the new blooms break forth. Sometimes those dreams return stronger and clearer than before, like Mom's roses that bloomed brighter after the hard pruning.

But I had to lay it all down – surrender and humble myself – for those dreams to bloom again.

Years ago, Dr. James Dobson spoke about a time when his son was a toddler and had a severe ear infection. The doctor had to probe inside that painful ear, and as the boy lay on the examining table, the doctor asked Dobson to hold him still. As the process began, the little boy looked into his father's eyes with tearful confusion. His frightened expression seemed to ask, "Why are you hurting me, Daddy?" There was no way to explain to the young child that this was all being done for his own good. Dobson's son only knew that his father was allowing him to go through deep pain.

I am thankful for a Father who prunes, because I also know He is the Father who protects and provides. There are many things I won't understand this side of heaven, but I know God loves me, and He protects my dreams.

Maybe you feel like an ugly winter stick – bare, vulnerable, and wondering when the time of pruning will end. I want to encourage you to hold on to the dream, and the One who put it in your heart. Don't give up, but instead, embrace the time of pruning. Your Savior has a green thumb, so rest in the assurance that spring is coming, and you are in the hands of the Master Gardener.

The Deep Release

I stood in the kitchen, making coffee, and thinking about trust. All my life I have known that trusting God is easy to talk about, but harder to do when the storms are raging. It was 2011, and my son Jordan had been home from college during Spring Break when he got news from a friend on campus. Someone had broken into his apartment and taken everything: computers, cameras, his guitars, and sound equipment, even his clothes. Also gone were his portfolios, books, and his childhood Bible with chapel and church notes.

My health struggles had demanded that I trust God in a deeper way, but this felt different. Watching my children suffer when it was out of my hands required a deep release. I always want to fix everything for my kids, but I couldn't bring back all that Jordan had lost. As a mom, I pray for my children daily, giving them over to the Lord and trusting Him with their lives. But when a crisis comes, I want to take back the worrying and hang on to my children for dear life. They are adults now and releasing them into God's hands is a necessary passage for our family. I find, however, that I'm forced to do it over again, and again, since I keep taking it all back when I think God isn't looking.

God has carried my children their entire lives and has never let them go. He never will, but that day I was tempted to pick up the worrying again and tote it around on my shoulders. That still, small voice of the Lord said, "Just watch." So, I did. I watched my son refuse to cry, yell, or get angry. He quietly turned around and went upstairs to pray. Jordan trusted God in the middle of this situation. It's humbling to watch your child display their love and trust for Jesus, even in the middle of a storm.

Jordan moved back to Oklahoma from Nashville to regroup and think about where he wanted to be. He decided to enroll in a different school, which required another level of trust to know that God would also be with him in a new place.

A few months later, I was sitting in a quiet house, thinking back on how God worked everything together for Jordan in this, for his good. I reflected on the past year, and how our circumstances had forced us to trust God in big and small ways. He lifted us up and over the hurdles, and other times He jumped over them with us. Sometimes He coached us as we faced unexpected challenges and cheered us on when we emerged on the other side, a little battered, but wiser. When it came to my children, He held them in His arms as tightly as a mother with her newborn child. His arms are everlasting and strong, and they continue to hold our family's future, and all our hopes and dreams.

He is with us through our questions and hurts, and is always asking, "Do you trust me?" I heard Him ask me that question throughout the weeks and months as we watched Jordan face the hurdles that came with losing so much. It wasn't easy, and I wished a hundred times my son would have been spared from the intrusion and injustice. But God taught me how good it is to release my children, a deep release that increases my faith little by little. Now I know He will never let us fall from His everlasting arms. And we can say, "Yes, Lord, we trust you with it all."

Learning to Lean

When I'm cleaning house, my mind sometimes wanders to memories of the past. One day, in the middle of mopping the floor, I was suddenly back in the third row of the church sanctuary, holding my baby boy and sitting next to my two-year-old daughter. It was Mother's Day, and I was trying to hold back tears. Gulping and taking deep breaths wasn't working well, and I feared ruining the service for everyone around me. Who wants to hear a lady blubbering on Mother's Day? But at that moment, I was overwhelmed by my circumstances, and worried that I might not have what it takes to raise my son and daughter alone.

This was my first Mother's Day as a single mother, and the enormity of this responsibility hit me in the middle of the church service. Relying on my own strength would not be enough for the journey ahead of me. It was during those years that I learned how to lean. I knew Jesus was the lover of my soul, my maker, and my friend. My relationship with the Lord had been solid since childhood, but this experience of parenting alone would take that relationship to a whole new level. God, through His amazing grace, walked me through one of the toughest seasons of my life, but I had to learn to let go and lean into Him. And there were days when I gave up and just cried out for God to carry me through the next five minutes.

When I think back to those days of exhaustion, loneliness, and uncertainty, my heart is burdened for all the single moms who are now sitting in the church pew, or the parent-teacher conference, or trying to get through the holiday season. These women are giving their heart, soul, and body to raise their children. There were days when I felt like I couldn't take another step, and yet my children were my highest priority. So, I put one foot in front of the other and leaned into Jesus.

I had plenty of questions for God: How did this happen to me? How would we put the pieces back together? Did God care about the little things that seemed so monumental to a single mom? Just packing the car for a play date took all my energy on certain days. I felt inadequate, and my self-esteem hit rock bottom. I wondered if God had forgotten my deep desire to be a mother *and* a wife.

That day, as I remembered those single mom years, I glanced over at a framed photo on my desk. My family had grown to include a wonderful husband, two more children, and three dogs. This photo was a daily reminder of how God had been faithful to this single mom so many years ago and continued that faithfulness by forming a new family. It seemed like a miracle when I thought about it. I dropped my mop and grabbed the photo, holding it to my heart. God had heard that young mother in the pew on Mother's Day, trying to muffle her sobs, wondering how she was going to provide for her children. He walked alongside her every step of the way and led her out into a new life that was far better than she could have imagined.

When I have the privilege of talking to single moms, I tell them there is hope, restoration, and grace for them. The road seems long and thankless, but it is a journey that leads straight to God's heart. He sees every tear you cry, hears the prayers you whisper in the darkest part of the night, and feels everything along with you. Even if the journey takes years, God never leaves you to walk the path alone.

Mothers are precious to the Lord. My prayer for all single moms is that you will glimpse the treasure you are, and know the journey is leading to a better place. There will be a day when you look back and smile at the miracles God brought to you. Keep looking ahead and hanging on to the One who will walk you through it all. Keep leaning into Him and knowing that you can fall into His arms. It's the best place to be.

It's Just Data

The day before my website launch, I heard the words, "It's gone, and there is no way to get that information back." The computer tech told me he had never seen anything like this before. My computer had crashed, data erased. Every tech in the room had been working to retrieve my precious folders and photos, but the data had vanished. Not even the cloud could help.

They almost needed to fetch a paper bag to keep me breathing. "The launch is tomorrow, and all the folders I needed were there, ready to go!" I said, not even trying to hold back tears. He shook his head. He was out of ideas, and I was a sobbing mess. I lost my data that day, which sounds like a sad country song.

The tech told me they would start over with what they could retrieve, but no one was very hopeful. I left my computer and drove home, pulling tissues from the box until it was empty. This was a king-sized pity party, and I finally prayed out loud. "Really, Lord? This had to happen now?" I was on my last tissue when the Lord grabbed my attention and pointed out that *this was just data*. "You said to trust me in the little and big things. Are you trusting? You didn't lose a child. You didn't lose a loved one. You just lost your data. You don't think I can fix data? Maybe I have a different plan at work here, so just be still and trust."

I got it. At that moment, I needed some perspective. Considering everything going on in the world, this was quite small. Perspective. We can look at the sudden, unwanted turns in our lives as annoying interruptions and let them tear us apart, or we can see them as divine disruptions. Often these are strategic times when God puts a "holy hold" on our plans and asks us to see them as blessings rather than curses. It's always safer to think we can hold those disruptions in our own hands, believing we can control the outcome (after our tantrums). But God asks us to trust Him with those annoying interruptions, and my ability to do that was put to the test that day.

At the stoplight, out of tissues and with my eyes swollen from crying, I let it go. God had this situation in His control. My data was in His hands, and if I never got it back, I was still going to be just fine. This was not my battle to fight. There had been too many lately, so I gave this one back to God.

The tech told me it would be weeks before my computer could be fixed, so when he called the next morning to tell me it was ready, I was sure there had been a mistake. I hurried to the shop and waited at the counter, hopeful, but still confused. The tech appeared, and he was smiling. "Lisa, you have all your data back. In fact, your computer is working better than before. I can't explain it. We put it back together and it was ready to send off for the mainframe to be replaced, but everything came on. Battery charged, ports working, even the glitches it had before are fixed."

I opened my mouth to say thank you, but all that came out was a squeak. I could barely breathe to get words out. After I carefully loaded the computer back into my car, I did the biggest joy jump ever. Some people might have their own explanation for why my computer miraculously started working, but all I could hear in my spirit was, *You just lost your data. Don't you think I can fix that?* It was not about data; it was about trust. The website launched on time after all, and even the stuck "A" key and spacebar were working!

Disruptions can take us out of our comfort zone and show us that God's handprints are on both the big and small things in our lives. Every moment I spend worrying is a moment when I miss the opportunity to trust that God can use everything to work His miraculous plan for my life. That day caused me to look at those disruptions differently. What is important? This is a question I must ask myself daily as each disruption comes at me. When I am focused on the mission and purpose, I can walk in freedom. But it is a choice I must make. I invite you to make that choice also. Take the pressure off, trust that God can handle the disruptions, and walk in the freedom He offers.

Heavenly Interruptions

I'm susceptible to earworms. You know how this works. One song gets lodged in your brain and tortures you for days, replaying in your head and sticking around even when you try to drown it out with something new. Sometimes you can't remember how the song got there. Maybe you didn't notice the department store music, or the tune that played while you stood in line at the post office. That was me with the old Julie Andrews song, *Favorite Things*. I spent three days listening to it.

Raindrops on roses, whiskers on kittens. It's such a happy little song and soon I was replacing the lyrics with my own favorite things. *Dogs in the backyard and Grandma's fudge candy. Porch swings in springtime and kids that sing dandy.* My lyrics weren't so great, but honestly, I was losing my mind a little.

It got me thinking about things I delight in. Depending on the season of life, those sources of delight may vary. What puts a smile on your face or brings light to your world? Delight is something that provokes pleasurable emotion, a deep sense of enjoyment, or a high degree of satisfaction. If we look around us, our favorite things are everywhere, and God will often use these delights to accomplish His will in our lives.

I have a friend who believes she can only recognize God's

voice in the desert or in dark times. She struggles to hear Him during the daily journey and only looks for Him during a crisis. On the normal days, she doesn't always feel His presence.

Trials teach and shape us, but they are not the only catalyst God uses to draw us back into His presence. God can be in the valley, or on the mountaintop, but He is also in every place in between. He speaks as powerfully during simple times of delight. I'm learning to not only reach out to God in times of disaster or when there is no place else to turn. Instead, I'm seeing Him in the simple delights, the everyday moments that make me smile. Most of our days aren't spent on the mountaintop or down in the deepest valleys. It's just regular life, daily tasks, workplace and home, cooking and playing with the kids or the dogs. Little delights come along, and God is there. I have learned to sense God's holy presence in the places I routinely visit and be open to the surprises He has waiting for me there.

God's voice is not echoing somewhere off in the distance. It's not thundering from the mountain peaks. He speaks to us in the daily moments and His voice can be heard loud and clear if we listen for it. The voice of God is most distinct in our delights, which is the place of praise. God provides us with the simple longings of our heart – the ones we rarely recognize as longings. What if we could see these simple delights as big heavenly interruptions, reminding us He is always with us, and for us? He gently hands these to us a hundred times a day, but they are easy to miss.

My favorite things are not always just things. They are God's reminder that He holds every piece of our lives – big and small, broken and intact. When I have a moment to enjoy time with my dogs on a sunny day in the backyard, it's a delight and God is in the midst of it, reminding me He loves to shower me with the desires of my heart.

These are heavenly interruptions that take me out of the here and now and transport me to God's goodness. This is the place where He waits, hoping I take nothing for granted. It's all part of the life He has given me, a blessing I can pass on to others.

I'm keeping my eyes and ears open for God in the simple delights of my day. And I'm thanking Him when I notice them, recognizing that these heavenly interruptions are some of my favorite things.

Ugly Crying in the Closet

I needed a cup of coffee before I looked over my tasks for the day, but after one sip, I felt an urgency to go check on my daughter. Kerrigan was recovering from a routine tonsillectomy, but the surgery had left her struggling and me worrying. The urgency to check on her grew, so I left my coffee and ran into the living room. What I saw made my heart race. Kerrigan was lying in a pool of blood on the couch, looking like she was in the middle of a crime scene, with streams of red running from her nose and mouth.

We rushed her to the hospital, where she underwent emergency surgery for an artery that had not been cauterized properly during the first surgery. It had opened, which caused the bleeding. I'll never forget standing in that hospital room, looking down at her frail, pale body after the surgery.

This was the same day my oldest daughter was leaving for Beijing, China, where she would spend the rest of the summer. Laura and I had planned to spend some time together before we said our goodbyes that afternoon, but in the span of 15 minutes, I had waved goodbye to two children – one as she left for the airport, the other as attendants wheeled her into surgery.

In moments like these, they tell you to stay strong, quote

scripture, pray, have faith. But as I stood in that hospital room with one daughter, knowing the other was heading to the other side of the world, I couldn't bring even one scripture to mind. And I didn't feel very strong. I was able to sputter three little words that I repeated over and over: "Help me, Jesus." Those were the words on my lips as I moved through the terror of seeing one child covered in blood, and the heartache of knowing another was on a plane to China. Both things left me feeling helpless.

Was I strong? It depends on how you define the word. I made it through the day with a determined posture and an attitude of resilience. But when I got home, I found that special place in my house – a closet – where I cry in the ugliest way. Those are the cries that come from the gut, and groans that don't quite sound like words. It's amazing how Jesus always meets me there; in fact, he's always in that closet waiting for me to arrive, ready to open His arms and catch me. I let it go that day, once again releasing my children to God, but realizing sometimes I just need to remind God that this is really *hard*.

Kerrigan recovered from her surgery, and Laura made it to Beijing. And I realized that it's okay to let myself go and cry out to Jesus when I can't remember the scriptures or don't have the words for an eloquent prayer. He is there for ugly cries and gut groans. God knows the deepest longings and fears of our hearts, especially when it comes to our children. He is waiting to meet us in that place where we can let it all go and not worry about what anyone thinks. That day, the name of Jesus was enough, and His name will be enough tomorrow and the day after that. Our lives are a journey of staying strong by falling apart in His arms, the safest place to be.

Hard Seasons

Wheelbarrow Rides

As a kid, I never sat still long enough for my mother to read a book to me. When she was in the middle of a sentence, I would push her hand out of the way and turn the page so I could see the next picture. I'm still not an avid reader. I take a long time to get through a book, and I still like a few photos scattered on the pages. I'm a visual learner, and over the years I've had to remind myself that God created me that way. Some of us just can't stick with a long, wordy instruction manual!

God speaks to me through images. Many times, I've wished that I could paint on canvas what He shows me in my spirit. He uses those visuals to help me through the journey. One morning, I sat in a doctor's office, my heart heavy with the unknowns and my brain envisioning dark scenarios. The crowd in the waiting room also seemed anxious, and I think we were feeding off one another's emotions. I needed a different visual image in my head, a reminder that all would be well. As someone near me took a deep breath, one came to mind. It was an illustration I had heard somewhere, and it stuck with me.

A traveler hiking through the wilderness comes to the edge of a canyon. Seeking a way to the other side, he discovers a big rope stretched over the canyon. As his eyes follow the rope toward the other side, he is surprised to see a man coming toward him, pushing a big red wheelbarrow. As the man arrived on his side of the canyon, the traveler's eyes grow wide. "That was amazing!" he exclaims.

The man with the wheelbarrow smiles and asks, "Do you believe I can do it again?"

"Of course," the traveler replies. "You walked across that rope with such confidence."

The man asks the same question, "Do you really believe I can do it again?"

The traveler doesn't hesitate. "No doubt about it," he replies.

"Very well then," says the wheelbarrow man. "Hop in and I will take you across."

I can picture that scene in my mind's eye, and I see myself in the traveler's place. Many of us look at God like He is the man with the wheelbarrow. We say, "God can do anything," yet when it comes time to get in the wheelbarrow, our faith dwindles and we'd rather stay on our safe side of the canyon. That day in the doctor's office, I wasn't sure I could hop into the wheelbarrow and trust God to get me to the other side. My fears were taking over, and the rope across the canyon looked mighty thin. But God has never let me down, and I've seen enough of His promises fulfilled to know that I can trust Him to carry me across.

In that doctor's office, I was determined to get in the wheelbarrow and thank God for His faithfulness. That was a big step out of my comfort zone, because most of the time it's easier to focus on the worst potential outcome. Those images will loom large until we take control of them. When God asks us to trust Him, that means He is with us, steering the wheelbarrow, no matter what the outcome. He's got us, even when we're on a thin rope!

In the waiting room, as we were packed in like nervous sardines, I prayed for everyone around me. We all needed some peace. When my name was called an hour later (I had lots of time to pray), I pictured myself climbing into that wheelbarrow and gripping both sides, my eyes wide open for the ride across – the first of many.

God has continued to be faithful over the years, and I've sat in quite a few more waiting rooms, waiting for my ride. And every time, when I remember who is steering me on this journey, I look around and am amazed at the beautiful view that surrounds me.

Looking Up from the Valley

My friend and I sat together while she talked about a lone-liness that seemed to loom around every corner. It left her feeling like she was sinking. My friend, who had recently been diagnosed with stage 4 cancer, was in a deep valley, and having a hard time looking up. Tears streamed down her cheeks as she asked, "Is there any way out of this valley?"

After she shared how broken she felt, we sat in silence. My heart was hurting along with hers, so I held her hand and whispered a prayer. I've heard the word *valley* many times this year, and several of my friends know the place well. I've also been there in the past months and found it hard to pick up the pieces of my brokenness and climb out. During a recent valley, I asked God to reveal what He wanted in this season. Why had I landed there? What was the purpose? It wasn't long before God met my cry with some answers, but I understood my friend's feeling of loneliness.

You can't plan valleys or add them to your schedule. They come out of nowhere, often at the worst time. Is there ever a good time for a valley? I'm reminded how God assured Moses that he would be with him when it was time to lead the Isra-elites to the Promised Land. God said, *My presence will go with you, and I will give you rest* (Exodus 33:14). I like Moses's reply in verse 15: *If your Presence does not go with us, do not send us up from here.* I agree with Moses. When I am going to unfamiliar places, I want God with me. It's comforting that He never asks us to go through valleys alone.

One of my favorite promises is in Psalm 23:4: *Even though I walk through the darkest valley, I will fear no evil, for you are with me.* David fought giving in to fear during those dark valleys. Earlier in the Psalm, David refers to God in the third person in verse 1: *The Lord is my shepherd, I lack nothing. He makes me lie down in green pastures, he leads me beside quiet waters.* But in verse 4, when David gets to the dark valley, he switches his language to first person: *For you are with me.* In this verse, it gets more personal. David sees a dark place ahead, and he reaches out for God's hand. That's an intimate picture of how God wants us to regard Him when we are in the valley. We can reach out our hand for Him without hesitation, knowing He is close and ready to walk the unfamiliar path with us.

I'm learning how necessary the valleys are. There is preparation within them, and a stretching space. They change our perspective, and while we are there, God leads us to new levels. He transforms the valleys into a gateway of hope. God is the God of valleys, and He does strategic, purposeful work that can only be accomplished in that place. The valleys help us appreciate the mountaintops that we have experienced – and will experience again. The valleys are temporary, and within them, God doesn't waste the pain. He uses it to take us to a higher place.

As I walked beside my friend through her cancer journey, I watched her reach a hand out to God many times, and each time He led her to a beautiful place. She told me she felt closer to her Savior in this valley than ever before. She walked through a valley, and, like David, referred to God in the first person. *You are with me.* God is holding her, and someday she will look back on this journey from the top of the mountain. She and I talk about valleys and mountaintops a lot these days. Mountaintops are wonderful, but valleys are merciful places where we learn to hold God's hand. We need both, but we especially need the assurance that He has already traversed the valley ahead of us. As we finished our coffee and were about to say our goodbyes, my friend looked at me with a tear in her eye. "Lisa, I'll take this valley with Jesus any day over a mountaintop without Him."

I couldn't have said it better.

Kintsugi

I stood at my kitchen counter with a delicate white bowl in front of me and a hammer in my hand. The tiny piece of ceramic looked too beautiful to break, but that was what I was here to do. After taking a few deep breaths, I began. The first pound of the hammer cracked the bowl in half. I continued with another blow, more breaking, and a large piece fell to the floor and shattered into even tinier pieces. I finished with one final pound and looked at the fragments scattered across the counter and on the floor. Just a few minutes earlier, the bowl had been a useful container, and now it was a broken mess.

Kintsugi is the ancient Japanese art of repairing ceramic pieces with gold, leaving the reconstruction visible as a symbol of fragility, strength, and beauty. Like ceramic, people can be strong, but we can also break. Kintsugi teaches that broken objects are not something to hide or throw out, but to display with pride. There is strength in brokenness.

Before I lead others in making this art, I wanted to prepare by breaking and repairing my own bowl. I thought this practice session would be interesting but not particularly emotional. I was wrong. It took a while to work up to breaking my bowl. I spent time admiring its beauty, and when I could finally land the first blow, tears welled up as I watched it fall into two broken halves. I didn't expect tears, but with each pound of the hammer, and more breaking, emotions welled up in me from deep places. It was as if every fresh break represented a place of brokenness in my own life, and every time I heard shattered ceramic hit the counter, it reminded me of the jagged, sharp edges of loss, hurt and betrayal. After I finished, it was no longer a bowl, just like the broken times in my life that have made me feel like I was not a person, just a raw, shattered soul with her pain exposed.

I wiped my tears and continued the process.

The next step was to use a special glue and gold that would repair the pieces and make the bowl whole again. I stared at the mess on my counter, certain it couldn't be done, but as I smeared the shimmering epoxy on those broken edges, even the jagged pieces fit together. Not perfectly, but that wasn't the goal. The gold made up for the places where edges didn't come together easily. A unique work of art was happening here. The cracks were still visible, but now they were beautiful. After I glued the final broken piece into its place, I stood back and looked at my bowl. Lots of emotion rose to the surface as the process reminded me of my own broken places. Each gold crack was symbolic of the cracked places in my life. This past year, I walked through a deep, wrenching blow of my own. I didn't see the hammer coming down on me, and it shattered me to my core. The breaks felt irreparable, but this experience of Kintsugi made me realize pieces that had appeared hopeless to repair were the places where the bowl looked more beautiful. It took more gold filling to repair the largest cracks, and their beauty drew more attention. As I looked at my repaired bowl and all the gold cracks winding through the ceramic, I thought about the recent blow that forced me to walk through a broken place. There had been pain, but also resilience to bounce back, repaired and shining again. God had done this work with me during the past year – repairing, healing, walking me out of brokenness and into purpose.

Part of that healing included forgiveness, love, praise, gratefulness, community. They were all like the gold epoxy, mixed to form a bond that will not shatter so easily next time. I am stronger in the broken places, because of the broken places!

God used that pain to teach me life-changing lessons, including forgiveness. It shines like gold and fills the biggest cracks. Forgiveness and love go hand in hand. God's redeeming love is bigger than your enemies and His love is always redemptive. Have you been abused, insulted, betrayed, lied to? Do you feel shattered? If so, let go of the anger or unforgiveness. There is freedom in forgiveness, and it allows us to see beauty in the cracks. After you allow forgiveness and love to repair those broken places, praise and gratefulness will follow. There is praise in knowing that God restores what the enemy meant for evil. There is praise in redemption.

Communities of grace bring healing. Through my own broken place this past year, I recognize more than ever how important a healthy community is. And I'm now able to better identify unhealthy communities. Walking out of my brokenness has made my vision clearer, and I can see God revealing to me how important it is to be with genuine souls who have pure motives. A healthy, inner circle of friendships and community help heal our broken places. Who is your community? Are they building you up or tearing you down? Are their motives pure? Is there gossip and slander? Are they praying for you? Healthy community is part of the gold glue that holds us together.

If you are looking at broken pieces of your life and wondering when redemption will come, don't give up. Keep hanging on because God has work to do with those broken pieces. If you allow Him, He will repair your brokenness, and create a beautiful masterpiece with your life. This is the promise of Romans 8:28: *And we know that in all things God works for the good of those who love him.*

Do you believe your broken places are beautiful? Trust that God has all those pieces and is waiting to fit them back into place, cracks gleaming like gold, resilience shining, preparing you to walk out of brokenness and into purpose.

Burned Bridges

"If a friendship ends, it was never a friendship to begin with."

I read this quote, and at first, I nodded in agreement. But it also got me thinking about a friend who was grieving over a broken relationship, and the conversation we had about her pain. "It feels like someone died," she said through her tears. They had been friends since childhood and knew everything about each other. She said the anger made her feel like a bridge had burned, and that realization broke her heart the most.

It was not the first time I had talked with someone in pain over a broken relationship. I've been there too, and had to put my mom's favorite quote, "Love wins," to the test. When we can't get across to one another because of burned bridges, hurt runs deep.

On a trip many years ago, I boarded a ferry that would take me to another island for a sight-seeing excursion. As the boat approached, I watched a young lady who was waiting for someone. She was restless with anticipation and excitement, and as soon as the boat arrived and the bridge lowered, she ran to greet her friend. It had been years since they had seen one another, and the look on each of their faces was pure elation. That bridge brought a joyful reunion. As I talked to them, they described a relationship that had been through difficulties and conflicts that could have resulted in burned bridges. But through the peaks and valleys, their friendship had remained solid.

If a bridge is burned, that means both sides have been destroyed and I must accept my part in that destruction. When someone hurts me in a relationship, I ask myself if I burned the bridge, or did I forgive and keep my side of the bridge intact? Love and forgiveness go hand in hand, but there were times I wanted to hold on to the anger. "Forgive? Really, God?" His answer is always "Yes." It takes so much more energy to be angry than to forgive. When I try to stay mad, I just end up exhausted.

Mom always said that "Love wins" is a lesson about forgiveness. It's about taking the burden off your shoulders and freeing yourself to love more deeply, even if the person never comes back. If they choose not to forgive, to hold back love, or stay angry, they have destroyed their side of the bridge. We can love them despite the burning, however. That act of love frees us to pray for them with an authentic heart that desires healing for all of us. And if there is an opportunity for the relationship to be restored, your side is ready to welcome them across again, like the bridge that brought the two friends back together for that joyful reunion.

In my own strength, it is impossible for me to love and forgive this extravagantly, but one of my favorite quotes says it best: "Man's extremity is God's opportunity." These places of hurt are His opportunity to move in and work miracles, even when healing might only be for my heart. But He is faithful. Life has forced me to put this kind of forgiveness to the test many times, but God hasn't let me down. Even if I never see love reciprocated and the person burns their side of the bridge, I feel peace when I forgive, love, and pray for that person. This allows me the freedom to move forward. When we love deeper than we thought we could, our love bucket overflows, and on the tough days, I need to draw on that love to get me through.

I think the quote should be, "If a friendship ends, love doesn't." Love wins, even when the bridge looks charred and beyond repair. Don't give up, because God is a master bridge builder, and His bridges stand the test of time.

Praising Through the Dust

My friend Emily worships in a different way than everyone else around her. With her wheelchair positioned at the end of the row, she can move freely, her arms waving in the air with abandon, her face glowing. She sings at the top of her lungs and doesn't care who is watching, or what they are thinking. She doesn't care if she's off-key or behind the tempo. This is Emily's time with Jesus, and she savors it. This young woman has faced many hurdles in her life. Emily's body is 17 years old, but her mind never caught up and is still at a seven-year-old level. I love watching Emily because she doesn't worship to impress or please people and isn't worried about religious styles and rules. Out of childlike trust, Emily gives Jesus everything she has, and her face radiates love.

Praise and worship are not just about singing, but about living, loving, and getting through tough times while still acknowledging Who is in control. Like Emily, I can leave behind the rituals and styles and remain in a state of worship wherever I am, any time of day. Even in a fetal position on the floor. This is the place of trust, knowing the only way I will get through the darkness is by hanging on to God and allowing myself to be intimate and vulnerable.

I love this quote from Alicia Bruxvoort: "Trust doesn't sprout in the absence of doubt. It grows in the presence of relationship." Psalm 9:10 says: *Those who know your name trust in you.* Knowing God grows trust in God.

A while back, I experienced a day of unusual worship when I couldn't raise my voice or hands. I couldn't even stand up. My body was curled into a fetal position on the floor after experiencing one of the deepest betrayals of my life. It came out of nowhere, and I found myself unable to speak aloud a calming prayer or a soothing scripture. But from the depths of my pain, I whispered a song.

Lying on the floor, singing a praise song in a barely audible voice, is an unusual way to worship, but it counts. A moment of brokenness became beautiful as I stayed in that most intimate place with the Lord, where nothing else mattered. God can hear our voices if we're raising it to the rafters, or barely getting the words out while lying on the kitchen floor. He is wherever we are, taking delight in the kind of worship others might question.

That day on the floor was one of the most beautiful moments with my Savior. When you feel broken into the dust of a million pieces, it seems impossible that God could put those pieces back together. As I sang the words that day, I realized God would use my dust to create something new. Every challenge can be a starting place. I did not lose all hope but trusted the hands of the Potter to create something glorious from dust.

Are you shattered? Have you lost your song? Maybe it feels like your purpose is hidden. Dare to believe you can trust God with your dust. Know that you can place your life in the hands of a Potter who will never let you break beyond repair. We can see our brokenness as unfair or as a necessary ingredient in creating something new.

When words fail and your heart is breaking, you can whisper a song on the floor, or belt out an off-key verse. It doesn't matter. Find that song in your heart and sing it softly, or like Emily, with wild abandon. Let God have your brokenness, knowing that something new, healing, and beautiful is waiting on the other side.

Waiting and Soaking

"The doctor can see you in January," said the voice on the other end of the line, and my phone became slippery in my hand from a sweaty palm. I was certain I had misheard.

"But that's seven months away."

"Yes, it is," said the too-chipper voice on the other end of the line. "We look forward to seeing you!"

I sat down in disbelief. I felt deflated and defeated, so I threw myself a pity party, complete with tears, questions, and grumbling. It had taken me two months to get this referral, and now I faced more waiting.

I hear from so many people who are in "the waiting" season. It's the part of the journey that can be both exhausting and frightening, especially when it concerns health issues. We want to rush forward and fix whatever is wrong, change our circumstances, resolve the problem. I always wish for an easy way through it, but there isn't one. God is constantly teaching me during those waiting times, reminding me to trust Him through each slow-motion step.

After hearing I was in for a seven month wait, I sat in my closet – the place where my most fervent prayers usually take place – and tried to pull myself out of the frustration and accompanying pity party. A steady rain was falling, and I heard every drop hit the roof above my closet. I let myself feel the rhythm. It was comforting, and as I quieted myself, I heard God speak to my heart: *Lisa, just as you are listening to the soaking rain outside, soak yourself inside my presence and rest.*

Rest and wait.

I do neither of those two things well, but sometimes they are the only responses to what lies ahead. I looked around my prayer closet that day and read the scriptures on the wall. After reflecting on my vision board for a while, I began singing my favorite praise songs. The sound of the rain was a comforting backdrop, and I leaned into the moment and steadied my breathing. Many years ago, when the drip of Mom's first chemotherapy treatment began, she had also started singing.

"Turn your eyes upon Jesus, look full in His wonderful face."

Even though she was battling fear, the words were soothing, and I watched the tension and anxiety leave her face. They were replaced with a sweet peace. "And the things of earth will grow strangely dim, in the light of His glory and grace."

Mom was living out those words in the moment, and she closed her eyes and smiled. She was waiting on God and resting in His promises. Mom didn't know how long the wait would be or what result was coming at the end, but her response was to soak in God's presence, even on one of the toughest days of her life.

As I sat singing that same hymn in my closet, every breath became a little easier. I felt peace move across my body and I decided to soak in God's presence instead of resisting the wait. James 4:8 says: *Come near to God, and He will come near to you.* I could wallow in my pity party, or delight in the desires God put in my heart, trusting that He would bring them to pass in His timing. Did I believe Psalm 37:4? *Take delight in the Lord, and he will give you the desires of your heart.* Yes, I believed it, but I had to make the choice to let that truth change how I felt about the waiting.

I could either endure the day or enjoy it. Enduring the day meant I would fight against every challenge and obstacle. Enjoying it meant I would use the hard moments to remind myself of blessings and God's promises. Instead of cursing the wait, I could celebrate the day. Maybe even bring out the party hats! Waiting is a battle, but it wasn't my battle to fight, so I gave it over to God and tried not to take it back. He wanted to fight that battle for me, and He was already on the other side of the mountain with the answer. I had to trust Him to get me over this mountain, and my negative outlook only delayed the journey.

In that quiet moment of soaking, God showed me that cleansing myself from the worry, anxiety and stress would replace it all with rest, relief, and peace. Once again, I experienced the restorative power that comes when I choose more of God and less of me. He knows what's on the other side of that mountain. The answer is there, if I will allow the things of earth to grow dim, rest in His promises, and soak in His presence during the wait.

Between Soon and Now

My friend's hand trembled as she lifted her coffee cup for another sip. She was walking a heartbreaking journey, and I could relate. Hurt. Betrayal. Feeling blindsided. People she loved had wounded her heart, and she was carrying the pain around, wishing she could drop all the baggage. But the wounds were deep, so we shared our stories, cried tears over our coffee cups, and prayed that God would bring comfort and healing. On my way home, I remembered how desperate I was to hear from God after a betrayal. We've all walked through those moments when we've cried out, "Lord, please help me NOW!" They are dark valleys when you want "soon" to become "now".

Waiting for answers during painful times is like a slow transit to a better place. It just never moves fast enough. But the only way to reach the "now" is to wait, pray, and leave it in God's hands. Our circumstance can become a magnificent picture of God's grace and our faith in His promises, but it will happen in His time. During the most difficult waiting times, reading James 5:11 gave my heart a lift: *As you know, we count as blessed those who have persevered. You have heard of Job's perseverance and have seen what the Lord finally brought about. The Lord is full of compassion and mercy.*

"God will bring an end to this," I told myself during the hard seasons, but until that time my job was to settle, persevere in hope, and trust that God was growing necessary patience in me. I'm "patience-challenged" and waiting for closure always exposes my level of faith and trust. It's not always where I want it to be. Waiting has also revealed the shape of my character, and sometimes I fail miserably, stomping my feet and pleading for the pain to end.

I have learned that God is always working in the time between "soon" and "now". He is the potter and waiting makes us moldable in His hands. He works the wet clay and forms an adult from the child in me that wants everything in my time, which is usually now. While He is molding me, He is also teaching me to act while I wait. I don't put everything on hold until that prayer is answered and darkness has passed. Instead, I cast my cares on the Lord while I continue living, loving, serving, and walking in trust. He takes care of the rest. I've uncovered miracles in the "soon" moments, and I've realized that the waiting is the most fruitful time.

I met up with my friend again to see how she was doing. There were no tears during our time together, just smiles. She had walked through the pain, and God met her in the "now" with healing. I felt a sense of peace as I listened to all that God had done in her life as she waited for the clouds to lift, and the clear skies of healing to return. What she experienced during the waiting made her "now" moment more precious. I was not surprised when she told me that the peace she felt was beyond what she had dreamed. God is good at giving far more than we expect or deserve.

When I want "soon" to be "now," I remember that God blesses those who persevere through the long days, months, and years of waiting. The Lord will bring about exactly what we need when we need it. Press on, friends. He is faithful.

Dog Days

Earl the Pearl

The smell of cigar smoke told me Mr. Earl was near, and before long, I could hear his loud mumbling. My elderly neighbor reminded me of Walter Matthau in the movie *Grumpy Old Men*, but Mabel always perked up when she saw him coming. She would pull on her leash to catch up with him, and I'll never forget the first time Mr. Earl noticed her.

In his cranky voice, he gave her a nickname: "Fluffernugget with Weird Hair." His voice was raspy and followed by a cough, then an announcement to me that he cared little for dogs. I didn't believe him. His eyes softened when he saw Mabel, and she picked up her step when she saw Mr. Earl. There was more to this cigar-smoking, gruff old soul, and I was confident Mabel would help me find it.

One day, Mr. Earl was walking slower than usual, cigar smoke swirling above his head. We hurried to catch up with him, and when we did, Mabel leaned her furry body into Mr. Earl. This is her favorite way to show affection, and she looked up at him with her big, white-toothed Mabel smile.

"Well, Fluffernugget with Weird Hair, how are you?" He stopped and gave her head two quick pats. I had never seen Mr. Earl smile, but Mabel's leaning forced him to crack a grin.

I handed her leash over to him and he walked with Mabel on one side and me on the other. She pranced a little, proud to be by Mr. Earl's side, as if they were old friends.

As we walked, I asked Mr. Earl how he was making it through the pandemic. Was he doing okay? That question was all he needed to open up and tell his story. Mr. Earl, my gruff neighbor, had served in the military and lost friends. His battle stories were heroic, but he wasn't bragging, just sharing the heartbreak of loss, including losing his wife when he returned from service. I began to understand why he had grown a tough exterior. He had lived a hard life, and he was battle-worn. Mr. Earl blinked a few times when he talked about losing Gus, his beloved old mutt he rescued from the side of the road one day. He saved Gus, but Mr. Earl said the truth was the old dog saved *him*. The two of them were inseparable during the years when Mr. Earl was losing people he loved. And then, Gus was hit by a car, and Mr. Earl was left without his beloved companion. He was alone.

"I guess I wasn't being truthful when I told you I didn't care for dogs," Mr. Earl said. "I just hate losing them." He shook his head. "Gus saved my life, and saying goodbye to him was a tough blow, and I'm a tough guy."

Mr. Earl told me when he felt anxious, old Gus would lean into him like Mabel. We walked on for a few minutes, and then he turned to me and said, "I think Fluffernugget with Weird Hair knew I needed some calm today, and a little laughter."

He told me this day had been hard. Another dear friend had died, and he was going to another funeral. Mr. Earl was tired. As we walked, I saw past that rough exterior and into the soft, tenderhearted part of Mr. Earl. There was a sweet, kind spirit, hidden under the frowning face, grumbling voice, and cigar smoke.

When it was time for the three of us to part ways, Mabel gave him a wet kiss on one of his hands.

"I kind of like you, Fluffernugget with Weird Hair, and I think you like me too." He gave a thumbs up and thanked me for listening to his stories.

As Mabel and I walked home, I thought about the commitment I had made two years earlier to meet my neighbors, get to know them, and pray for their needs. The story of how a pearl forms had been the focus of one of my devotionals that week. A tiny sandstone finds its way under an oyster shell, irritating it so that it begins to work on the stone. After months, sometimes years, the sandstone becomes a smooth pearl. Pearls are costly and precious, and it takes many of them to make one necklace.

I think Mr. Earl was like that pearl. In fact, I gave him the nickname Earl the Pearl. On the outside, he was cranky and tough, as if he hated the world and everything about it. But inside was a man with a story of love, loss, heartbreak, and resilience. His bravery and heart to help others were beautiful. Like the pearl.

Jesus told the parable of the merchant looking for fine pearls, and how it is like finding the kingdom of Heaven. When the merchant found one, he sold everything to purchase it. Our salvation is like that pearl because nothing is more valuable than security for our souls.

On our walk the next day, Mabel wore the pearl collar that had once belonged to my first therapy dog, Mavis. I put a small pearl I had tucked away for safekeeping in a mesh bag. The pearl came from an oyster I received many years ago and was the perfect gift for my new friend. We saw the plume of cigar smoke, and Mabel ran to Mr. Earl. He pointed at her pearl collar and commented in his gruff voice, "Little Miss Fluffernugget with Weird Hair is all decked out today!"

I told Mr. Earl she wore it just for him, and I handed him the bag with a pearl inside. "Your story matters," I said, and I told him the parable of the pearl, and that God had a purpose for his life. "Your life is like this precious pearl."

He pulled out a worn handkerchief and wiped his eyes, then bent down, and instead of giving Mabel his usual two pats on the head, he held her face in his hands. "Fluffernugget with Weird Hair, I think you have the heart of my Gus. I kind of like you."

Mabel had known that inside Mr. Earl's rough exterior, there was a gentle soul. A pearl.

Mr. Earl moved away eventually, but I pray every day that he will remember he is a soul of great worth. My encounter with Mr. Earl caused me to look at pearls in a new way, and to be careful about judging someone before my dog weighs in. They say diamonds are a girl's best friend, but I'll take the pearls.

A Walk with Mabel

Mabel and I began our usual daily walk, but something different happened that day. We were a few houses down from where we started, and Mabel halted without warning. She stood completely still and wouldn't move. This dog never halts, so I was waiting to see what had caught her attention. She looked at the house, looked at me, and then continued walking. The next day, Mabel made the same sudden stop. I was baffled at this unusual behavior, but I have learned to trust my dogs. They know things that continually surprise me.

As we pass each house, I pray for our neighbors, their homes, and families. For several days, Mabel halted in front of the same driveway, stared at the door, looked at me, and continued. One day, despite my best tugging efforts, I couldn't make her budge. We made it to the end of the street, and she planted all four paws and sat. She glanced at me, and then looked behind her, down the street at that same house. I was trying to figure out what was going on with Mabel, when a truck pulled up beside us. As we stood there, Mabel looked at the driver, then at me. I waited and watched as the vehicle's window lowered. It was a neighbor I had become friends with, and I instantly knew something was wrong.

"He's gone, Lisa," she said.

It took me a minute to realize "he" was her husband. She had lost him to COVID and I'm sure my face reflected shock as she told me the story. The week before, the three of us had a long conversation, so it didn't seem possible that he was gone. My neighbor, with devastation and shock in her eyes, filled me in on the details. It had happened suddenly, and she wasn't allowed into the hospital room with him. He breathed his final breath alone. That made the loss feel deeper, and she told me she would never stop imagining the loneliness he felt at the end. As my neighbor drove away, Mabel watched the car disappear, then locked her eyes on mine. I could almost hear her saying, *I stopped so you could pray.* Suddenly, I realized she had been refusing to budge in front of this neighbor's house, watching the front door, and waiting for me to do something before she continued.

How do dogs know these things? I'll never be able to answer that, but their sensitive hearts inspire me to pay attention to the world around me. What if we could open our eyes to the hurting world in front of us and be ready to pray in our busiest moments? We can't always know what goes on behind the closed door of people we care about, but God does. And maybe we need all the help we can get with this, which is why I think God gives us dogs. Sometimes, they can sense things we are too busy to notice. Now, when we walk, I don't drag Mabel along if she is determined to stop. I take a hint, and say a prayer for my neighbors, and the world beyond.

Grace Days

The animal emergency center was almost full on a Friday night, and I sat on the last plastic chair available, waiting to find out if our new puppy, Maddie Grace, had ingested the squeaker in her toy. I didn't know whether to laugh or cry as I waited on the X-ray. I wanted to see the humor in it, but the worry of whether she would be okay was at the forefront.

All the worst-case scenarios ran through my mind as I paced the exam room, flustered, and mumbling under my breath. This was not the place I wanted to spend a Friday night, and not the frame of mind I needed to be in after a long week. I paced for ten minutes then sat down on the bench and took in the quiet of the room. "Oh Jesus, I need some help here," I prayed. "I'm tired. My head hurts. I'm worried about my dog." Mental and emotional exhaustion made my body feel wrung out, like I had nothing left to help me handle the moment.

In the stillness of that room, I took a deep breath, and could almost hear God whispering to my heart, *Lisa, take a grace day.*

What is a grace day? I loved the way it sounded, and I closed my eyes and imagined an entire day all to myself. God already knew. I needed to stop, listen, rest, and remember that His grace is sufficient to carry me through worries crowding my mind. I had been trying to be strong for others, and a grace day would allow me to release all the tensions I had been holding inside.

Then I began to argue with God, even though I knew all of that was true. "But Lord, I already do that!" It was humorous – me debating with God about taking a grace day. I needed a *lot* of grace.

I am willing to give it to everyone else, but it has been hard to give grace to myself. In that moment, I realized that to walk in His grace, I needed to stop and take a breath. People like me often hold emotions and feelings inside, so we can charge through the tough stuff. We keep going even when we're exhausted and overwhelmed. Stopping feels like giving up, even though the stillness is where we find the voice of God. He calms every storm and all my worries. The more grace days I take, the more clearly I will hear the Voice that leads, reassures, encourages, convicts, and comforts me. I can release the emotions I hold inside straight into His hands.

Maddie is now "squeaker free" and we're all happy about that. After my night in the animal emergency room, I took a grace day. It felt wonderful to give myself permission not to rush, but to let God take all the worrying scenarios from me. While I didn't plan to spend my Friday waiting to see an X-ray of a squeaker in my dog, I came away from it with a new awareness.

It's okay to give yourself grace, so take a grace day! (And schedule it if you need to.)

Because soul care is important.

Freaky, Fabulous Fred

I met Frederick the dog on one of my daily runs. I know his name because I heard the neighbors calling for him one day, but I renamed him Freaky Fred. He was a spastic rat terrier who seemed to plot ways to sabotage my runs. The little dog would pop out the moment we passed, barking and nipping at my ankles, and causing me to fall on my face a few times. Fred also loved to torment my dogs, and once hopped on Holly's back when she passed him. The dogs would look at me a few houses before Fred's as if to say, "Please don't make us run past the freaky little dog's house!" We tried to change our running route, but Fred always found us. After a while, I became bothered that the owners didn't seem to care about controlling their annoying pet.

I began to avoid Freaky Fred by taking a different route where he couldn't find me. One morning, I was running without the dogs and enjoying the solitude when an elderly man in a car rolled down his window and waved me over. He looked distraught and when I got to the car, I noticed he was crying.

"Miss, I know you run in our neighborhood, and we've lost our dog. We've looked for a day now and can't find him." He described his lost dog and, you guessed it, he was looking for

Freaky Fred. I'm sorry to admit I was a little relieved there would be no more falls and tormenting of my dogs from Fred. But that passed quickly as the man wiped his tears and glanced around for another look. I told him I would help search for his dog.

I was off my regular route, and certain that Fred wouldn't be anywhere close. Reluctantly, I prayed for Fred and as I did, my heart got a little mushy for the dog. I became determined to find him, which had to be God, since any other day the prospect of facing Fred would cause me to run the other way.

About three miles into my search, I looked over and noticed movement in a bush. I slowed and walked over to get a closer look, and there was Fred. The little terrier was shaking and covered with mud. He was no longer the rowdy dog who wanted to take on the world, but a frightened, vulnerable creature who looked up at me from behind a bush.

"Okay Fred, it's just you and me. I know we haven't been the best of friends. In fact, I've detested you a tiny bit, but it's time to change that." In the past, Fred was always in attack mode and would never let me get close to him, so I slowly held out my hand and waited. Fred peeked his dirty face from the bushes and leapt out like a piece of popcorn, bypassing my hand and landing in my lap. He licked my face as if to say, "I'm sorry and I surrender! Let's be friends!" At that moment, Fred and I became buddies. It was about three miles to his home, and I held that little dog the entire way. During our run, we sort of bonded, and I realized that Fred had a story. I didn't know it, but I was about to find out.

As I walked up the hill with Fred in my arms, the older man was standing in his driveway. When he saw me with his dog, he put his hands on his cheeks and, in a quavering voice, called out, "Is that Fred? Do you have our boy?"

I waved to him triumphantly. "Yes, I found him!" I felt a

catch in my throat and a tingle in my nostril, but tried to swallow back the tears. The face of Fred's owner did me in, and I began to cry. We must have been quite a sight – a sweaty, sobbing woman trudging up the hill holding a muddy little rat terrier. When Fred caught sight of his owner, he jumped out of my arms and the reunion began. The humans cried, and the dog barked for joy. As I talked with Fred's owner, the story unfolded. The man was caring for his wife, who had Alzheimer's. When the couple rescued Fred the previous year, he had cuts across his body and raw, bleeding rope burns on his neck. The couple saved Fred with good intentions of training him, but health issues prevented it. The man and his wife had been too overwhelmed to help him learn manners and how to ignore the passing runners. Despite his many quirks, they loved Fred. When he went missing, the wife was distraught. She couldn't imagine what she would do without their little dog. As I walked into their backyard, I saw the small hole where Fred would make his daily escapes. The man was too busy caring for his wife to realize Fred had slipped through the fence and was roaming the streets. Together, we secured the escape route and then I looked at Freaky Fred and he looked back at me. I learned the man had named Fred after his brother, and at that moment, I knew that little dog and I would stay friends. Hearing the man's story changed my heart.

I spent several hours with the couple that day, and then ran home, thanking God for the lesson of Fred. He was "freaky" for a reason. His tough exterior covered up some deep hurt and pain, and his attacks were a type of protection for him. All along, Fred had been trying to communicate his story in a very canine way. "I've been hurt, and I won't let you hurt me. In fact, I'll get you first!"

How many Freds are in your life? How many times have we

judged others without knowing their story? When people hurt or mistreat us, we often label them as mean, rude, or hateful. We've all name-called others who are different and rub against us like sandpaper. They may be family members or people we encounter in passing. When someone hurts me, I am guilty of this. I disregard them as hopeless, and leave the situation annoyed or angry. I don't stop to consider that sometimes, a person simply needs a kind word, compassion, and time to tell their story to someone who will listen. Like Fred, some people tremble in the bushes and cover the hurt with a tough exterior, until they can't anymore.

After my encounter with Fred and his owners, I asked God to give me eyes to see and a heart to love the people who hurt me. Instead of labeling them freaky, I need to remember that in God's eyes, they are fabulous! I continue to pray that God will clear my vision, so I can see people as He sees them.

Fred now watches me through the gate window when I pass his house on my daily run. I've renamed him Fabulous Fred, and I smile when he wags his tail at me, then I walk over for a quick pet and chat. One or two days a week, I leave my dogs at home and I walk with Fred. During our time together, I've trained him a little and realized that he is a smart fella. We are best of friends now, and I've deepened my relationship with his owners as well. A few months ago, I couldn't have imagined Fred and me hanging out, but God has a way of turning Freaky into Fabulous!

Think of people in your life who annoy or hurt you. Ask God to change your heart toward those people and you'll be amazed how the doors begin to swing open. The change will always begin in your own heart, and blossom from there.

Divine Detours

"I missed our exit!" I said aloud to Mabel Joy. "How is that even possible?"

We make this drive often, but today I felt distracted and after missing the exit, we found ourselves on a grand detour. I glanced in the rearview mirror at Mabel Joy, who also seemed distracted. Most of the time she sits patiently in the back seat, but today she was up and down, looking out the window, unable to get settled or relax.

"Great. A missed exit, a nervous dog, and now I'm going to be late."

In the middle of my grumbling, I noticed a car in front of me stopped in the middle of the busy street. A little further in the distance, a white lab swerved in and out of traffic, dodging cars and in danger of getting hit. I slowed the car, certain this wouldn't end well. The frightened dog was not only running from the cars, but from everyone who tried to catch her. Her frantic state kept her darting back out into the middle of traffic. Another car missed hitting her, and I pulled to the side of the road, not realizing I had rolled the window down. The dog was headed my way, and in my frazzled state, I forgot Mabel was in the back seat. I saw an opportunity to get the dog to safety.

"Oh Jesus, I need my dog to bark. Bark, Mabel Joy! Please!"

I was pleading for a miracle because our Mabel does not bark. Since we have owned her, she has only squeaked what sounds like little chirps. But I didn't need chirps. I needed a loud, excited bark to coax the wayward dog in our direction. As it weaved back out into traffic, I turned and saw Mabel's head sticking out of the window. Now I realized why she had been pacing and seemed uneasy. And then, I heard it. A loud, commanding bark from the back seat. Not just one, but a beautiful stream of staccato barks. My dog barked as if her life depended on it. As if the life of that beautiful white lab depended on it!

I jumped out of the car and kneeled in the middle of the street, praying that the white lab would hear Mabel's barking and come to me. She stopped, listened, and ran straight for me and into my arms. I took her to the car and looked into her eyes. She reminded me of Holly, my therapy dog who had passed on. My legs shook like limp noodles, and I took deep breaths to calm myself.

Her frantic owners ran over, tears streaming. Someone had accidentally left the gate open, and she got out. They talked fast, relieved but still shaken. "How did you get her to come to you? Nobody could catch her! It's a miracle you were here!" After I returned the dog to her grateful owners, I got back in my car and sat for a moment, feeling flustered. I turned to Mabel and her big brown eyes were watching me, waiting.

"Mabel, you barked!" I said joyfully. She looked content and happy with herself, no longer pacing and anxious. I was so proud of her.

As I sat behind the wheel, not quite ready to pull back into traffic, I realized the prayer I pray every morning had just played out in front of me. "Lord, let nothing I do today be an accident. Orchestrate every single step."

I missed an exit, took a detour, and God used us to help save this dog. And Mabel Joy barked – a miracle itself! Too often, I have complained about missing an exit, taking a wrong turn, facing an annoying delay or an unwanted detour. But that day, I was reminded that it is in the unexpected roadblocks where we are most likely to encounter teachable moments and miracles. Things may not always go according to my well-laid plans, but God has greater plans waiting that I could never have imagined.

I need to remember to relax, even during the unwanted detours, because that is where we often find preparation, re-flection, new perspectives, miracles, and rest. We can rest in the detours if we choose to see them as opportunities. Detours are not derailments. Delays are not denials. God is still work-ing, and we are allowed to slow down and enjoy life. I love this quote: "It's not only the scenery you miss by going too fast, but you also miss the sense of where you're going and why."

The next time you miss that exit or encounter a roadblock that takes you on a detour, enjoy the ride. God has a bigger, better plan.

You Are Enough

"You shouldn't be here. You are not one of us."

I was coming out of the practice ring at Nationals where my golden retriever, Gracie, was preparing to compete. It was a miracle we were here, considering that the dog ring brought huge fears of failure for me. It didn't help that my sweet golden retriever could be wildly unpredictable. Leading up to this moment, there had been many times when we were escorted out of the ring after the dreaded NQ (Not Qualifying). The humiliating walk out of the ring was always in the back of my mind.

Those fears were looming large when the lady approached us with those hurtful words. She followed them up with a sentence that broke my heart: "You are simply not good enough at this."

What made this lady believe I wasn't good enough? I ran through the possibilities, my hands shaking as I held Gracie's leash. Did I train my dog wrong? Was the embroidery on my shirt not up to the standard? Was I wearing the wrong colors? The questions came down to whether I believed I was "enough."

Thirty minutes later, our time came to compete, and it was at this moment that one of the event photographers took a photo of Gracie and me. My face captures the pure deflation I felt – my head is leaned back against a wall, my eyes closed, mouth tight and tense. Gracie felt it too. The words, *not good enough, not one of us*, were playing on repeat in my head. I wanted to run and hide, but instead I had to walk my dog into that competition ring. I felt like there was a giant sign on my back announcing to the waiting crowd that my dog and I were not good enough.

"Are you ready?" The judge nodded at me. I swallowed hard and gripped the leash tighter.

"Yes, I am." That wasn't exactly the truth. I looked down at Gracie and her head was turned up at me with a look in her eye I had never seen. My sweet Gracie knew my heart was broken, and she was going to do her best to get me through the toughest competition of my life.

We hadn't brought a cheering section like many teams did, but I knew we had enough. God, my dog, and me. I felt love and strength, and we nailed that competition.

My husband greeted us as we walked out of the ring and wiped a tear as he whispered to me, "You don't want to be one of them, Lisa, because you are *you*. And there's no better you than you!" He gave Gracie and me a big hug. I didn't need a cheering section. The truth of those words backed up everything that had happened in that ring. Even if we had lost, we were still good enough.

I ran into that lady at the end of the competition and asked her what she meant by her comment.

"You have way too much fun in the dog ring," she replied. "You don't follow protocol. You are not one of us. We take our dog training seriously." She narrowed her eyes and added, "Weren't you the one that gave the judge a party hat in the ring after you won a ribbon in rally?"

I felt relieved. So *that* was my problem! Yes, I was the one who gave the judge a party hat, and we danced in the ring together. But what the lady didn't realize was the judge had just been diagnosed with cancer, and Mom and I wanted her to have a party hat like the one we wore during chemo treatments. I brought it hoping I would qualify with my dog in that judge's ring. We wanted her to know that she wasn't alone, and that we were praying for her. The judge wore that party hat and we danced together. It was a precious moment.

As I stood with the lady who believed I was not "one of them," I realized she was right, and I apologized to her for my frustration. She was even more confused when I hugged her and thanked her for giving me one of the best compliments I had ever received. She had provided a teachable moment with my dog.

Training my dog was about having fun and bonding. It was therapy, and if God wanted to use my dogs and me to minister to others, it was both a privilege and an answered prayer. The dog competitions were not about ribbons and medals, both of which ended up in a box in my closet. It was about the lessons I learned and the ministry of loving people with the dogs by my side. Those dogs have taught me more than any human ever has. Even the dreaded NQs were not failures, but opportunities to improve.

That day, I walked out of the ring with a ribbon, a happy golden retriever, and a lesson I carry with me. No competition, person, or opinion can change Who I belong to, my love for my dogs, and my desire to have fun and love people along the way. If all the dog training led up to that day and to the awareness that I was good enough and fulfilling God's purpose for my life, then it was worth it.

Since that competition, I have never entered the ring again with my dogs and have no plans to compete again. But the joy I had in training five therapy dogs and one service dog to spread love and joy to people has been so rewarding. I may not be receiving ribbons in the competition ring, but there is nothing better than seeing a child who has walked through trauma break into smiles and laughter because of my dogs. The comfort and joy they bring is the best award I could receive.

Remember Whose you are. Savor the moments and don't sweat the NQs in life. They will make you stronger and wiser for the journey ahead. *You are enough.*

What My Dogs Taught Me (So Far)

Two weeks ago, Mabel Joy was under my arm 24/7, which is exactly what I needed. Our family fought through COVID with our dogs never leaving our side – Mabel Joy snuggled against me, Maddie Grace next to Skipper. As I write this, Mabel has wedged herself beside me, as close as she can get. This makes me smile. She has stuck by my side through the past year, and as I look into her big brown eyes, I realize how much I've learned from my dogs. In no particular order, here are the lessons they have taught me.

Don't judge people.
We are so quick to make judgements based on outward appearance. Dogs don't do this. Everyone has a special story that is worth listening to, but when we're focused on nitpicking, we are the ones who miss out. My dogs are superb listeners. They've taught me that if we take our eyes off what people look like and listen to their hearts, we'll hear some important stories.

Dogs savor the moments and enjoy the journey.
Mabel and Maddie soak in every second of the day like

they are guests at the biggest party anyone has ever thrown. They focus on what's happening in the moment, not the end result, or what might happen in the next hour, tomorrow, or next week. They don't spend their time asking, "What if?" My dogs just roll with the twists and turns of life, no matter where it takes them. And they enjoy the journey–with a big tail wag and a smile!

Be genuine with your apologies when you are wrong.

We should not downplay our offenses or give half-hearted apologies. When Mabel lets me down, she lays at my feet and looks up at me, her eyes clearly communicating that she is sorry, and wants forgiveness. With her eyes locked on mine, I stay upset for about 30 seconds before I melt. I love her and trust her apology and we move on to the next moment. Imagine if we could sort out all our disagreements quickly through genuine apologies, letting go of grievances or extending true forgiveness.

Persistence pays off and practice makes perfect.

Training Mabel and Maddie to be therapy dogs has taught me how impatient I can be. Just ask my trainers! My dogs don't know the trick before we try it, and they don't understand what I'm asking them to do the first few times. But when we break the trick down into small pieces, every milestone is a victory, and they love those winning moments. My dogs don't beat themselves up if they don't get it right the first few times. Instead, they wait patiently for the next step, and hope for that delicious treat. It's okay to fail on the first try. We don't have to achieve perfection before we've learned something. Failure makes the minor victories even sweeter.

Dogs forgive and move on.

I do at least one thing every day that my dogs don't like. For instance, I leave the house without them, or get too busy to take them for a walk or toss the ball around in the backyard. But no matter how many times I disappoint them in a day, they forgive me. There might be a few minutes of moping and whining, but before long, they are back under my arm. And my dogs have made me more adaptable too. Those brand new $150 running shoes never hit the pavement before they became chew toys, but I got over it. In the end, petty annoyances – like stains on the carpet and mauled sweaters – don't break the bonds between us. Holding a grudge magnifies the unimportant and minimizes the significant. Relationships matter and being able to forgive frees us to fully enjoy them.

Dogs love. A lot.

It can be expensive and inconvenient to bring a dog into your life. You find yourself up in the middle of the night cleaning a smelly accident, or in the doggy ER because your new puppy ate the squeaker out of her toy. Those twice-a-night potty training adventures can make the next day seem a little foggy, but we put up with all the hassles because we love our dogs. And they love us. And guess what? That feeling of being loved unconditionally is worth the mess. I can be messy, too, so I make sure the people I love know how much they mean to me. They put up with me, so it must be working.

Every minute I spend with my dogs makes me a better person. Thank you, Mabel Joy and Maddie Grace, for being such patient teachers and loyal companions. You deserve all the treats!

Over the Rainbow Bridge

My dogs have always been my heart-healing, safe place on this earth. It has been my privilege to share Mavis and Gracie as they have been that healing presence for others. The two girls endured health issues together over the last months of their lives. They were soul sisters, joined at the hip, and even in their painful days, they endured it together.

We knew Gracie was leaving us as we watched her health deteriorate day by day. I was thankful for every second we had with her, even though it was heartbreaking to watch. When she took a turn for the worse, Mavis, who had been struggling as well, seemed to join her there. They were descending together, and I knew what was coming.

There are those long moments when God's grace carries us through and gives us the gentle strength to do what we never thought we could. God walks us through loss in exactly the way we need to experience it. Why am I so surprised when He continues to come through in these gracious ways?

Gracie and Mavis took their journey to heaven together on Wednesday, May 19, 2021. God sent our faithful veterinarian to help them say their goodbyes at home, in their favorite place, holding on to each other. This rainbow bridge crossing was peaceful and sweet, and that was comforting for me.

These two sisters served so many and touched more lives than I could have imagined possible. They taught me lessons that continue to carry me forward. Gracie helped me conquer my fear of getting in the ring and competing in obedience trials, and when I went into my prayer closet every day, she was by my side.

Mavis came into this world called to greatness and walked out her calling until her very last breath. She knew when the season of my own life changed, and that her calling was now complete. It was time to close that chapter, and Mavis was there to help Mabel Joy, our new therapy dog, step into the next one. Gracie and Mavis taught Mabel well, and Mabel added days to their lives. The three formed a bond that is hard to explain unless you watched it happen.

Mabel Joy was ready to carry on dog therapy work in the new season. God knew what was ahead, and He placed Mabel in our lives at just the right time. As the ambassador of Lisa Bain Ministries, she carries on a legacy of healing, serving, and blessing many lives.

I wrote this just a few hours after Gracie and Mavis left us, and it felt like part of our hearts were missing as well. But the two girls are finally free of the pain and struggle, and we are thankful they are released. As we stepped into a season of new ministry with Mabel, we carried with us the memories of our time with Gracie and Mavis. As those memories mingled with the sorrow, we said goodbye, knowing it was not the end.

Family Blessings

Two Fathers

My tears fell into the carpet as I lay on the floor sobbing. I was a teenager who felt overwhelmed by life, and my self-esteem had hit its lowest point. In the middle of my full-on meltdown, my dad opened my bedroom door, sat down, and pulled me into his arms. Dad cried with me, and then he began to pray. He didn't pretend to have answers or advice, so he asked Jesus to wrap His arms around me, just as he was doing. I will always remember how Dad's lips quivered as he prayed. In my fit of rage, he ran to my rescue. Jesus knew I needed an extension of God's arms to hold me up and He sent Dad. My earthly father sat beside me in the dark place to exemplify a Heavenly Father's love.

My relationship with God comes from the example of my dad, who adored Jesus and his family, and was never afraid to let that show, even when it meant sitting with his sobbing teenaged daughter on the floor. Dad loved me deeply, which made it easy for me to understand how a big God could love me with such tenderness. I saw that kind of love lived out every day in my earthly father. His role went further than just being a dad. He drew me to Jesus by loving me when I was unlovable and praying for me during my dark moments. When other dads might have fled, he held me close and trusted God to carry me through.

When I faced life alone as a single mom of a newborn and two-year-old, my father stepped in and took on a fatherly role (again), guiding, loving, and praying. My kids have a precious relationship with Jesus, and I give my dad much of the credit. He gave them that same unconditional love, support, and stability.

One of the most important gifts he gave all of us was the example of a deep, true love for my mother. He never spoke a cross word to her and knew their relationship was more important than petty arguments or selfish attitudes. Seeing his love for Mom kept me from giving up when my dreams of marriage shattered. He taught me to hang on, wait patiently, and trust God had a beautiful plan for my life. Dad reminded me that God wouldn't leave me and my children alone. The desire He put in my heart for a godly husband would come to fruition. Dad reminded me of this every day, and through his prayers and encouragement, it happened. I met and married the man of my dreams, and we blended our families. Dad never gave up on me.

The day my earthly father met me on the floor and held me in his arms, he taught me that when life hits hard, you move closer to Jesus. He lived this out through Mom's cancer journey, her death, and the loss he felt after she was gone. The choices he made in the hardest of times laid out a path for me to follow. I am blessed with a Godly heritage because of Dad. When people tell me how much alike we are, it's a compliment that sinks deep inside me.

So many people don't have an earthly father they can look up to, and many can't imagine wanting a relationship with a heavenly father. But God is the kind of father who will join you on the floor in the middle of the pain. He will hold you close and speak words of love. He isn't afraid of your worst days, and He won't turn and run when you are in the middle of a meltdown. I'm so grateful for that promise.

I'm no longer a teenager with low self-esteem, but I will never forget that day both fathers came to my rescue. It happened over and over. Arms extended, drawing me close and reminding me there is nothing I can do to lose that love. Dad pointed the way to Jesus, and I couldn't be prouder of the legacy he left to us.

No Longer the Same

In 2010, after a surgery that left me in pain and feeling a little depressed, I closed my eyes and pictured a woman with straight pins in her collar and boiled custard peanut brittle on the stove. Grandma Mabel kept pins in her clothes so she could get to them quickly when she was making little dresses to send with mission teams. And the boiled custard peanut brittle was a holiday tradition I looked forward to every year. It wasn't Christmas without it. My recovery had left me needing to feel a little bit of heaven and be reminded there is nothing too far away for the hand of Jesus. Not my pain, fear, or frustration.

I was stuck on the couch and working to take deep breaths – something my body had forgotten how to do since the surgery. I never thought breathing could be painful, so I was taking shallow gulps of air, which seemed to heighten the anxiety. I plugged in my iPod and a song came on. Did I put it there? I didn't remember adding it to my music library, but I was immediately taken further back to a time with Grandma Mabel in the kitchen around holiday time. The custard was on the stove, and she was humming. Ah yes, I remembered that hymn and the way she hummed it while she worked. The music sank deep into my soul, and I began to sing along with my iPod and Grandma Mabel. The song, *He Touched Me*, was a reminder that Jesus's hand is never far away, and when we lean into His touch, we are no longer the same.

I used to call these Old People Songs. They are the hymns tucked between hardbound covers we pulled from the back of the church pew every Sunday as we stood to sing together. Somehow, the words and tunes get lodged in our brains and then resurface often when we need them. I don't know how this works, but it does, and that day on my couch I was grateful this song came back to me.

I think my grandma was singing along with my shaky voice that day. A year of diagnosis, surgery, and recovery opened my eyes to the ways that heaven comes close to us. I was faced with how quickly our circumstances change and the fragility of life. The only way to get through it was to surrender. And that song reminded me that Jesus is close enough to touch, which means I can reach out my hand at any moment. And I did. I surrendered because I couldn't force my body to do anything. I had to be patient, trust God for the outcome, and rest in His touch.

I sang softly and carefully, still struggling with my breaths, and I felt my grandma humming and joining in on the chorus. I closed my eyes after the last line and filled my lungs with air. For a moment, breathing didn't hurt. Heaven had come close, and the healing touch was beginning.

We can hang onto God's promise that we will be made whole again, if not in this life, then in that heavenly realm as we sing with the angels. I grabbed that promise during my recovery and reminded myself of it whenever discouragement took over. He touched me. And joy flooded my soul.

There were still times when I wanted to give up, but then an old song would come to me in a moment, a reminder that God has given us words and music that bring Him close enough to touch. My grandma didn't have an easy life, but she held on to the promises and hummed the tunes as a gentle reminder to herself. When the hand of Jesus touches us, we are no longer the same. His touch gives us the strength to make it through another day, another surgery, more bad news and a scary diagnosis. I'm so grateful for the examples of the strong women in my life. They remind me that He is close. As I listen, I can hear the harmony of a thousand saints who also walked this road.

Keep it Simple

I climbed the stairs, as I do every morning, to pray for each of my children. I would go into their rooms after they left for school, and sometimes I would be there for minutes, or hours. On that morning, as I entered my son's room, I noticed an old typewriter on his desk. I stopped and stared. It was beautiful, with round keys and a sturdy metal body. Where, I wondered, did he get this gem? I later found out he purchased it for $25 at an estate sale, and I could only imagine the stories this old typewriter might tell. My grandmother owned one just like the one on my son's desk, and I remember typing on it as a child. The keys were hard to press, but I loved the little dinging sound when I pulled the silver handle at the end of each line.

I sat down at my son's desk, staring at this antiquated piece of equipment, and wondering why it gave me so much comfort. Surrounding the old machine was a computer, a television, and various other pieces of electronic equipment. But the typewriter seemed to send a message, and I leaned forward, looking at its worn ribbon and thought about simpler days. Although my kids can hardly believe it, there was a time when the phone rang, and we didn't know who was on the other end of the line. We spun vinyl records, and if we didn't like the song, we waited patiently for the next one – although sometimes we couldn't stand it and had to lift and move the needle to get past "that song." And phone cords kept us in the same room where we made the call – unless the cord was extra-long, allowing us to step around the corner for a semi-private conversation.

There were no computers, iPods, or social media, which left plenty of time to build forts, ride bikes, and play softball after school. Mom had dinner on the table at 5 p.m., and we gathered as a family every evening. At bedtime, my parents tucked me in and together we shared about our day. We prayed for the day ahead, and in those moments, Jesus seemed so close. Sometimes, when I take myself down memory lane, I lament the distractions that surround us.

And, yes, I'm typing this on my laptop while iTunes is playing praise music through my earbuds. I'm not against technology, and I am thankful the advances make life easier in so many ways. But I'm also challenging myself to focus on simple things that shape my life. I want to approach busyness with caution, remembering that each day is made up of simple things that also enrich us.

Just like that typewriter, I have many stories to tell, and many left to write. I want to savor the moments of each story, and I want Jesus in the middle of them all. When my eyes are on Him, instead of the distractions, He helps me see what matters. What is lasting here on earth and into eternity won't be the TV show, Facebook status, or cool song from my iPod. Those are all luxuries that exist in the world of distraction, and while I may enjoy them, returning to simplicity grounds me. I go back to the truth that "the greatest things in life aren't things." What matters is making time to spend with those I love – sharing stories, prayers, laughter, and quiet moments. I'm amazed how energized I am after being with my family or spending time alone with God. The world makes more sense, and I'm drawn back to Him for more of these priceless moments. He gives these gifts to us before we even ask.

Life hands us simple moments to savor, and when we take time to pay attention to them, we uncover hidden miracles. The more time we spend with Him, the more our hearts are content with simplicity and less prone to distraction. I'm learning to appreciate all the technology, but I'm also realizing God waits for me to join Him away from the noise, where real life takes place.

Silent in the Goodbye

I love my porch swing. It's one place I go to connect with God as I drink coffee in the early morning hours. The sounds of a new day, the frosty air, and the view of pine trees along the fence line remind me of God's presence. But then, sometimes there is silence.

Those pine trees at the fence line were perfectly still one day. Not a bird or a squirrel moved along the branches, as they usually do. It was almost eerie. I was trying to focus on my conversation with God, but my mind kept wandering and my eyes were drawn back to the stillness of the frost-covered trees. No movement. No sound. I felt like that tree mirrored my life at that moment.

How long, Lord?

When will you intervene?

Lord...are you there?

Everything seemed frozen in time, and I felt forgotten.

Last week, I remembered that day on the porch swing. We were losing Dad. He had been rushed to the emergency room, and we spent three days separated from him. God seemed to be completely silent, even as I cried out to Him to help me understand the "why" of what was happening. I reminded myself of the day I was watching those frozen trees and lamenting the silence. I had closed my eyes to plead for God's voice and opened them to see a brilliant blue sky, with white blobs of clouds sliding across it. There was a majestic mad dash of wonder above my head! Yet, there were the trees, frozen in time and unfazed by what was happening above. I had been so focused on the trees I had missed the sky. How could things be moving so swiftly over my head, yet in front of me the trees were immovable?

At that moment, I heard the still, small voice of Jesus sending me a message through those clouds. They were a visual reminder of His work in my life. I was so fixated on what was *not* happening that I almost missed what *was* happening. I may have pushed the "pause" button, but God hadn't. He had never stopped moving and working.

God knew when He would call Dad home, and He comforted my heart every time there was silence. God held my heart and poured out grace. I realized during the silence of that week and the grief of losing Dad, that God was most at work during the quietest moments.

My Bible study during this season was on Noah. He was not lost or forgotten in the great flood, but some days I wonder if he felt the silence. We read the stories in Scripture, knowing how it ends, and forgetting that these heroes of faith experienced emotions of living in real time. It's easy to assume Noah knew when dry ground would reappear, but Scripture doesn't give us that detail. God told Noah it would rain 40 days and 40 nights (Genesis 7:4), but how long would the flood waters linger? Can you imagine how Noah felt on day 57? Day 103? Day 148? He probably struggled to believe he would ever see dry land again. I would have! But God blew in at just the right time, sending a wind over the earth that caused the waters to recede.

Sometimes, the wind is all we need to settle our weary hearts and remind us that God is still moving in the silence. During the last week of Dad's life, when I was weary of that silence, God moved around us and above us. He kept me still so He could walk us through the entire journey and assure me that even in the silence, He is busy working on my behalf. If you feel the empty silence, ask God to breathe a reminder of His presence in your path. Quiet yourself and listen for His gentle whisper. You might not have a sudden end to your heartache, but it will be a reminder that God is working, and you have not been forgotten. His hand is guiding you, even in the silence.

Hands

"You have old people hands."

Art Linkletter was right. Kids say the darndest things, and sometimes those cute quips are painfully honest. My husband and I were sitting on a bench at an outdoor event when a little boy pointed out our hands and made his declarative statement.

We looked at each other and then back at the little boy. "What?" .

"Yep," he nodded, "you have old people hands."

As we looked at our hands with purple veins, age spots, and plenty of wrinkles, we had to agree. We intertwined those hands on the way home and laughed. Old people hands. That's us!

Not long ago, I saw a photo of my mom and I holding hands during her first chemo treatment and thought about how she used those beautiful hands to garden, teach piano, cook, clean, create, give. But it wasn't until the day Mom and I curled our fingers together during chemo that I realized the beauty of those hands, not because they were smooth and flawless, but because they had seen a lifetime of serving. Age spots and wrinkles were a testimony to what Mom's hands had accomplished.

I visited a precious mentor in the last moments before she met Jesus. The goodbye was heartbreaking, and I felt her squeeze my hand for the last time. This woman embodied the love of Jesus and spent her life giving and serving others. As I looked at her hands – wrinkled, frail and scarred from fighting disease, my tears fell. Those battered hands were beautiful. My friend had many reasons to fall into depression, discouragement, or hopelessness. Instead, she chose to spread love and encouragement, and she used her hands to bless and give to everyone around her. She replaced her worry with eyes that looked out instead of within. Her hands had carried so much for me this past year as I walked through grief and loss. She loved on me when she could have been taking care of herself. Those same hands I now held in these last moments of her life had wrapped around me during my darkest days, praying me through it all.

As I drove home that day, I glanced at my hands on the steering wheel and thanked God for the wrinkles and age spots. My mother and my mentor taught me so much about what it looks like to never allow my hands to be idle if there is someone who needs blessing and encouragement. Our hands are designed for this.

And those nail scars. Can you imagine how beautiful Jesus's hands were? I thanked God that day for the sacrifices He made for me so I could be at the bedside of my friend, and for all the moments that led me here. God's hands hold, fight, and protect us, and they gently pick us up when we fall. They put us back together when we are broken and lead us on paths we could never imagine.

Every day, I think about how I'm using my hands. They may not look like the hands of a younger me, but I don't care. I want them to be used for God's glory – to help a friend in need, or offer fellowship, comfort, and service. If God keeps me safe in His hands, how could I waste the opportunity to use the hands He's blessed me with?

Therefore, my dear brothers and sisters, stand firm. Let nothing move you. Always give yourselves fully to the work of the Lord, because you know that your labor in the Lord is not in vain (1 Corinthians 15:58).

Christmas Banking

I like to get my Christmas decorations early. Yes, I'm the person you might frown at when she purchases her tinsel and ornaments before the scarecrows and pumpkins are off the shelf. During one busy holiday season, I stood in line with my cart of Christmas purchases and tried to ignore the lady in front of me who kept turning around in disbelief. The line was long, and I wasn't looking forward to twenty minutes of her judging my basket of items.

In fact, everyone around me seemed to be cranky about the long line, and they probably thought my early holiday purchases were unnecessary. A man and woman nearby grumbled about the store Christmas trees being up and lamented the tragedy of skipping over Thanksgiving. I wished for a blanket to throw over my cart of red and green. Maybe it was too early. What was wrong with me anyway that I couldn't wait to get into the Christmas spirit? I'm the person who puts her tree up on November 1 and pulls out the Michael Bublé Christmas album before Halloween.

As I stood in line, I thought about the memories of past Christmases. Some were better than others. As a family, we had faced health battles and loss during the holiday season.

I remembered struggling as a single mom, determined to be cheery with holiday joy despite my circumstances.

Growing up, Mom and Dad made sure Christmas centered around Jesus, and one year they announced we would skip gifts and take the money we had set back for the holiday and give to a family in need. They made the announcement in early November, and I'd like to tell you I danced around with glee over the news, but I didn't. I pouted and begged, but also felt something stirring when I saw a single mother and her four children open their gifts and eat the meal we prepared. We put up her tree and helped her kids decorate it. I don't think Mom and Dad knew what a life-changing year that was for me, and how it redefined how I thought about Christmas. Something clicked into place, and I wanted to keep this spirit throughout the year.

Decades later, my daughter and I were chatting about the Christmas season while she worked on a math problem. She looked over at me and said, "Mom, I think people need to learn about Christmas banking. It's not about the purchasing, but the investing. You know, not so much about getting gifts, but giving." We talked about it for a while and concluded that Christmas is only as consumer-driven as we make it. The season should be about investing in the lives of other people, which doesn't always fill the room with wrapping paper and boxes, but it fills our hearts with something eternal. These are investments in the Kingdom of Heaven.

A few weeks later, Skipper and I announced to our kids we would celebrate Christmas without purchases. It would be about investing, like the year that changed my life as a teenager. I thought my kids would react the same way I had all those years ago, and I braced myself for the response. But instead of protests, they surprised me, and agreed to the change.

"Let's make new traditions this year. We'll give handmade gifts and celebrate with a homemade brunch!" The creative ideas were flowing, and I ran for the Kleenex. It was the first week of November, and instead of hitting the stores, our family was brainstorming ideas about how not to spend money. We put up the tree early, but that year was about investing, not purchasing. The tree was a necessary reminder that we had entered the season and were leaving behind the commercial hype to embrace a simple way of celebrating.

I thought about this as I stood in line, my cart filled with decorating purchases. No matter how we celebrate, we can remember Christmas is about the One who invested His life for us. I left the store that day with a renewed perspective and smiled at everyone around me. Yes, I was into the holiday spirit earlier than many, but putting up our family's tree was a reminder that it's a joy to celebrate the gift of Jesus. It's an even greater joy to turn around and invest our lives in other people, and that investment can continue throughout the year. Christmas banking makes sense.

Grateful Moments

Don't Forget the Details

Ida and Burton are always holding hands when I see them in our neighborhood park. Sometimes, she sits on his lap as they relax on their favorite park bench, gazing into each other's eyes like two teenagers in love. Ida and Burton are in their nineties, but it's obvious the romance is still there.

The couple's eyes lit up when Mabel and Maddie and I walked up to greet them. Mabel held out her paw for a shake, and there was an instant connection. For a while, we talked about the dogs, then I began asking them questions. I discovered their ages: Ida, 91 and Burton, 93. They have been married for 71 years, and I couldn't resist asking them their secret. How does one stay in such deep love for over seven decades?

Ida and Burton looked at each other and shared a quick laugh. "It's about the little things," said Burton. "We never forget the details. The little details. The hugs, the pats on the backside – the good ones, you know." He gave me a sly grin and a chuckle. "The little notes of love left here and there to remind each other that we kind of like each other." He winked. "It's about knowing there was never an out. There was always a way through." He added, "But we could never have made it without the good Lord. Many times, *He* was our way through.

We simply would not be here without Him. He took care of our details and helped us through every one of them."

Mabel and Maddie sat, as if they were listening carefully, mesmerized. And I was too! Ida patted Mabel tenderly on the head, while Maddie sat at Burton's feet. There had been many twists and turns in their lives. They lost children, and other dear loved ones, and they almost lost each other. The trials also included fighting for our country, facing cancer and COVID. At one point, they spent years apart because of military duties. I also learned that Ida was a musician who loves to sing and play hymns. When I asked her what her favorite hymn was, she began to sing before I finished the question.

Blessed assurance, Jesus is mine. Oh, what a foretaste of glory divine!

Her eyes were shining as she sang the words. I joined in because it is also one of my favorites. I told her I wrote a blog post about the hymn. "In fact," I said, "my mom and I sang it on the way to chemo appointments. It takes me back to a precious place."

Ida smiled. "Those are the details that matter. It may have seemed small, but that was something very special you remember, and you smile when you recall it. That's what we mean when we talk about the little details. Sometimes it's those details that keep us grounded when the storm winds blow. The details matter to us, and they matter to our good Lord."

I will never forget the stories we shared, but the biggest takeaway from that afternoon was the importance of small things. Over the long haul, they are the glue that holds a relationship together. God is in those small details, reminding us they always matter. He loves details! I looked back at Ida and Burton as I began walking home. They were holding hands, and I could hear them singing. They were living in the moment, savoring those small details. I pray I can remember how to live that way when I'm in my nineties!

God arranges those small details of life into a bigger picture to help us work our way out of hopelessness. Ida and Burton were a picture of how hopeless can turn into purpose. We may not see the big picture yet, but He sees it, and every detail matters. We have the "blessed assurance" of knowing those small details are leading us into a wide, expansive view of the plan God has for us. The picture emerges slowly, over time, and one day we will look back and see that there was always a way through. *He* is the way through.

Safely Sheltered

The slight chill in the morning air motivated me to unpack my box of fall clothes. With excitement, I pulled out my favorite sweatshirt. It's so old that the material is soft and worn in all the right places and when I put it on that day, it was like melting into a warm fuzzy. I now wear that sweatshirt each morning when I go into my prayer closet.

I snuggle in my prayer chair wearing my old sweatshirt and both make me feel like I am tucked inside a safe place. The moment reminded me of Psalms 91:4: *He will cover you with His feathers, and under His wings you will find refuge; His faithfulness will be your shield and rampart.* That sounds like a safe place to land!

There is a story about a mama hen found in the remains of a burned down chicken coop. She didn't survive, but the farmer found all her tiny chicks safely sheltered and alive under her wings. I love that image, but as I sat in the safety of my prayer closet, wearing my comfy sweatshirt, the world outside doesn't seem so safe. The news is devastating, medical diagnoses of people I love are heartbreaking, and there is a fear of what lies ahead. These days, I feel like one of those baby chicks who needs shelter from the fire raging around me. We can't deny that we are broken people in broken bodies, living in a broken world. Biting our nails or pacing the floor will not change that reality.

In those moments of feeling the world's brokenness, I am so grateful for the Word that reminds me I am tucked safely under the wings of my Savior. And the good news is there is room for all of us under these wings! From there, we can claim the truths found in His Word, knowing that we can stake our lives on them. In my prayer closet today, I soaked in the scriptures that remind me of refuge. *God is our refuge and strength, an ever-present help in trouble. The Lord Almighty is with us; the God of Jacob is our fortress* (Psalms 46:1;7).

These fears we live with in our broken world are not unfounded, and suffering will come. But we can run to Jesus and find that safe place in His presence. He wants to gather us like the hen in the fire and hide us until we are safe again.

Fannie Crosby wrote the beautiful hymn "Safe in the Arms of Jesus" in 1868.

Safe in the arms of Jesus,
safe on His gentle breast,
there by His love o'ershaded,
sweetly my soul shall rest.

Fannie knew about fear and suffering. She was blind from birth and faced many trials throughout her life. But she found safety in the darkness as she wrote over 5,000 hymns, many declaring the faithfulness of God. She said this, "Do you know that if, at birth, I had been able to make one petition, it would have been that I was born blind? Because when I get to heaven, the first face that shall ever gladden my sight will be that of my Savior." Fanny spent her life in darkness, but she was never alone. She was tucked safely under the wings of her Savior.

In His presence, we're overshadowed by love. So sweetly, our souls can rest.

I am thankful that the voice of my Savior welcomes me every morning as I enter my prayer closet. It is a safe place to land, where grace flows, the spirit refuels me, and where mercy covers my fear and stress. In this place, I can realign my priorities and take a deep breath. I am safe in the arms of my Savior, and you are too.

Take a deep breath and know that you are covered. You are safe.

Dream Big

On my walk each day, I pass an elementary school playground where kids are running or walking around a loop during gym class. I can't help but overhear their conversations, since many of them are loud and excited. I'm not trying to eavesdrop, but I love what I hear sometimes.

"My teacher said I would be a great writer one day!" a brown-haired girl waved her hands in the air as if she was writing in the sky. "She told me to dream big, so I'm going to write fun books that will make people happy."

The boy walking beside her laughed. "No way. You won't be a writer. That's dumb, anyway." He trotted ahead of the future writer, shaking his head back and forth.

"Wait and see!" the future writer responded, and I wanted to pump my fist in the air, both for the little girl and the teacher who had encouraged her dream.

The exchange took me back to elementary school, and a special teacher who impacted my life. I hated to read. Mom said I would never sit on her lap long enough for her to finish a story at night and would almost never pick up a book on my own. My library teacher, Mrs. Howell, noticed my intense dislike for reading and pulled me aside one day.

"Lisa, *you* are somebody, and reading will open your eyes about how to be an even better somebody." She took me over to a row of books and talked to me about what I was interested in. Dogs, I told her, and she told me to choose a book that matched my interest. I ran my hands across the row of books and pulled out one with a yellow cover. The author was Fred Gipson, and the title of the book was *Old Yeller*. I didn't care about any of that, however. I knew this book was for me because it had a dog on the cover. It was the first book I read from start to finish, and it still holds a place in my heart. *Old Yeller* was a tear-jerker, but so often, those are the books that help us gain empathy and maybe help us be a better somebody – in the words of Mrs. Howell.

I'm forever grateful she took time for that little elementary school student with the attention span of a gnat. She knew I needed a little push, and a reminder I was somebody who could read and dream.

The little girl on the playground was convinced she could be a writer because her teacher had believed in her. She was somebody! When the naysayers came around, she stood firm, and kept dreaming big. God instills dreams in us even when we're young, and those dreams may grow and change as we grow and change. Sometimes, we lose heart, wondering if our dreams are too big or crazy. We might believe we're not good enough to fulfill that dream or wonder if we got the dream wrong.

When the going gets tough, we aren't sure if the dream will ever come to fruition. Maybe it wasn't God's will after all, or we misheard our own heart's desires. We don't like waiting, but sometimes our dream is deferred because we first need to navigate through the tough seasons of preparation. It sounds like a cliche to say, "Don't give up on your dream," but we have enough voices coming at us that sound like the little boy on the playground. "No way. That's dumb." Often, we create these voices ourselves, and our big dreams get lost while the voices grow louder.

The waiting seasons are important to prepare us for our dream. Those tough times bring strength, vision, and purpose and move us closer to it. All the pieces, even the painful ones, are necessary.

I met up with Mrs. Howell later in life, after I dreamed some big dreams, and God brought them to fruition. I thanked her for planting a seed in my life 47 years ago, and for introducing me to *Old Yeller* and the joy of reading. And I thanked her for believing in me. Her eyes brightened, then she repeated the words she said to me in that elementary school library. "Lisa, you are somebody, and I am so proud of you." I'm not a little girl anymore, but her words made me stand a little taller, and know that I can keep dreaming big.

Feel the Rain

In the middle of an Autumn rain, she stretched her arms out and lifted her head to the sky, trying to catch every drop on her face. A few minutes earlier, she had been stomping in puddles, making sure she didn't miss one. It didn't take long for me to realize this child and I had different perspectives about the moment. I passed her on my run, but instead of playing in the rain, I hurried to make it home without getting drenched. As I stood in my kitchen, breathing heavily, and shaking water out of my hair, I thought about the Bob Marley quote, "Some people feel the rain. Others just get wet."

I wondered if I am the person who just gets wet. It's easy for me to be so busy with life that I forget to stop and savor the present. Every second we live is a moment that passes, and we often let them slip by without even noticing. Now that people are getting out and the pandemic has lessened, busy is busier than ever.

I was reading in my devotional about living in the *present*. Even the name declares how precious it is, and now I'm curious about how "the moment in time" came to be called the present. Could it be God's plan, because the present is a gift to be cherished? The present isn't wrapped in glossy paper but made up of small moments. In fact, those moments can seem so insignificant that we allow the world to distract us from them. We miss out on opening the present.

It's been a joy to watch our puppy, Maddie, prepare to become a therapy dog. Socializing her is an important part of the process, so I take her out to explore the world. I get to see her experience all the "firsts." Some of those first moments make her apprehensive, but soon she is jumping and feeling joyful about the situation. During those moments, she is savoring every rain drop.

As we begin a new year, new moments are waiting. The present will be before us as we take a step into 2022, and I want to be there for every one of those moments. I want to soak them in and savor their beauty. God shows up with surprises, and even the most mundane moments can be filled with "presents" if we look closely.

I want to see the world the same way that little girl felt the rain. She didn't waste any of it, and she certainly wasn't too busy to miss the joy. What if we all looked at our days with that kind of glorious anticipation, ready for every moment, not willing to waste even one. We just might find joy and praise, even in the struggles. What a present that would be!

Your life is filled with presents. What will you do with them? I'm ready to live in every moment, soaking and savoring, even if I get a little wet.

Behind the Seen

A precious friend and I shared a hug, knowing it would be the last time we would see one another. Literally. She was scheduled for surgery, and after she came out of it, her eyesight would be gone. Cancer had robbed her of vision, but it couldn't take away her smile as she opened the care box in front of her. It was filled with items she would carry along on the tough journey ahead. My friend wrapped herself in the handmade prayer quilt as tears rolled down both our cheeks. We hugged, and I reminded her of the impact she has made in my life.

That visit stayed with me and changed my perspective on what I see every day. It's easy to take for granted the blue of the sky, the color of a cardinal, people going about their day. But now, tones seemed more vibrant and sounds clearer and more distinct. My senses had been bumped up a notch.

I cried out to God on behalf of my friend, and as I prayed for her, He brought another friend to mind. Jenna had also lost her sight, yet I could walk into a room quietly and she would greet me. "Hi Lisa! I see you!" And then her beautiful laugh would begin. "I know you are there!" Her senses were so sharp. She had lost her sight, but not her vision. Jenna and I talked about the mountains in life we climb. Hers was losing her sight, one that I couldn't imagine.

"Mountains are not leveled overnight," Jenna said. "Crooked paths with their twists and turns are not suddenly made straight. God can send miracles that will make our paths smoother, but it seems He mostly chooses to combine His miraculous touch with our persistent prayer, and a little elbow grease!" Jenna continued, "Losing my sight was not at all what I had 'envisioned,' but what I gained was a clearer image than I had before. God has given me 20/20 vision! I see Him more clearly now and feel His presence stronger than ever. Was I disappointed at first? Yes, of course! I was distraught and heartbroken and filled with questions. But what was ahead of me on the road was an outcome I couldn't have imagined. God saw the mountain, and instead of me going around it, we climbed together. I guess you could say God was behind the 'seens' working for my good all along."

Jenna shared her story over and over and told it with such passion. She is a vibrant person who has touched countless souls by sharing her journey. If you talk to Jenna, she will tell you she found her purpose through that difficult time and discovered treasures in the darkest of places. She now focuses on those treasures and shares them with others.

On the drive home from my care visit, I thought about my friend who was facing a surgery that would take away her vision. I wondered how I was looking at my mountains. Did I view my circumstances the way Jenna did? We can either look at our mountain with God in the background or look at God with the mountain behind Him. If God is in front, we gain a crucial perspective on our problems. But if God is in the background, the hard climb ahead of us dominates our vision.

I am learning to flip the lens, realizing that God is behind the "seens" in ways I can't fathom. As I look at God in front of my mountain, my vision is 20/20. And as I look back on those mountains God and I climbed together, the outcome was better than I could have dreamed. The lessons learned on the mountain path changed my perspective, my vision, and my heart.

I will give you the treasures of darkness, riches stored in secret places so that you may know that I am the Lord, the God of Israel, who summons you by name (Isaiah 45:3).

Long Haul Friends

It was one of those afternoons when the world felt far away. Time didn't matter, because my friend and I were sharing stories, crying, hugging, and then laughing so hard we had to come up for air. We were cherishing our friendship under the warmth of an afternoon sun and the background noise of our dogs playing. We could have stayed there for days and still not told all our stories. It was perfect. I spent the drive home thanking God for the precious friends in my life, and realizing that those deep, inner circle relationships are rare. Those kinds of friends accept all your imperfections and don't vote you off the island when things get messy. They cry during the loss, celebrate after the victories, and hang with you through every ugly season. These friendships include not just talking, but listening; not just receiving, but giving. They bring joy to life and show us what it looks like when love is "lived out loud." That means that the bonds are often forged through pain, and through sharing moments that knock us to the ground.

I recently had coffee with a dear friend who was grieving the loss of a friendship. She was asking *why* and *how* as she sorted through the hurt of what had happened. This friendship was so dear to her that losing it made her feel like part of her identity was ripped away. A friendship that had once been beautiful was now broken.

These conversations keep coming around. For many, the pandemic has brought difficult friendship issues to the surface. What happens when a friendship ends? How do you navigate through that loss of trust and identity? These conversations help me reflect on the past year and cause me to realize there are friendships that only last a season. As much as it hurts, I'm comforted knowing my identity in Christ doesn't change. My worth is not determined by having an abundance of friends, but by the abundance of Christ's love for me. The same is true for you. I read about a pastor who told his congregation, "Christ is the light at the end of your dark tunnel. And He's not going anywhere. Others may leave, but He will stay." *He will stay.* Through every chapter of your story, He is there, never leaving or forsaking you.

The broken friendships in my life – even the betrayals – have provided important lessons for me to hang onto. I now know that my heart may break, but my vision becomes clearer, and the truths that are revealed can set me free. I am grateful for those friends who came into my life for a season and those who remain for the long haul. Both are necessary. What I learned in the broken places helped me discern what is healthy and unhealthy in a relationship. The lessons also allowed me to see how precious those deep, inner circle friendships are. I pay closer attention to how I can nurture and develop relationships that last more than a season.

It takes time and vulnerability to heal broken trust, but the journey through those dark places is so worth it. If you are grieving the loss of a friendship today, I want to encourage you. Through the hurt and betrayal, God is there, and He hears you cry out from the broken place. He is the Friend who never leaves. As He wraps His arms around you, He will point you toward the friendships with the laughter, tears, hugs, and stories. The friendships that stand the test of time help restore broken trust and give us a beautiful place to land when we feel like giving up.

I no longer call you servants, because a servant does not know their master's business. Instead, I have called you friends, for everything that I learned from my Father I have made known to you (John 15:15).

A man of many companions may come to ruin, but there is a friend who sticks closer than a brother (Proverbs 18:24).

God has said, 'Never will I leave you; never will I forsake you' (Hebrews 13:5b).

I, the Lord, do not change (Malachi 3:6a).

Alone in the Crowd

In the middle of a local coffee shop, I watched a swirl of people come in and out and felt a wave of loneliness settle on me. I had just finished visiting a family who is facing illness and tough decisions, and their words kept ringing in my head: "It's such a lonely journey." Their pain was profound as they encountered numerous battles around this illness. I have heard the word "lonely" many times during these past two years of pandemic, and with the virus surging again, even more people are telling me how alone they feel. In that coffee shop, with people all around me, I could relate. The unknown can make us feel like we're stranded on an island with no way to escape. I closed my eyes and took a deep breath as I prayed for this family and all who are walking through sickness and heartache. As I finished the prayer, I exhaled and whispered the name. *Jesus.*

I thought about the loneliness Jesus faced as the disciples turned and left Him. One by one, the people He trusted deserted Him, and in anguish He cried: *My God, my God, why have you forsaken me?* (Mark 15:34). Jesus experienced loneliness all the way to the cross, and then the ultimate separation from the Father. This is why I can bring the hurt to Him, and trust that He feels it with me on a deep level. He cares infinitely more than we can know.

Because of the sacrifice Jesus made, you are never alone or separated from His presence. *Never will I leave you; never will I forsake you* (Hebrews 13:5). As I sat in the coffee shop letting the wave of loneliness pass over me, the words of this verse surrounded and settled my soul. Never is a long time, but this verse gives us a promise we can hang on to. These are the moments when God is most real to me. He reminds me I can come to Him with my secrets and heartbreak, knowing His ear is tuned to my voice. God wants to listen to my long list of complaints. When I don't have the strength, He helps me forgive those who hurt me. When I am tired, He fights the battles for me. As I sat breathing a prayer for the family whose illness brought loneliness, I also asked Him to remove the blinders so I could see the situation as He sees it. I needed that clarity.

Are you feeling alone? Abandoned in your situation? No struggle is too big for God, and no situation is off limits. He wants us to bring the loneliness to Him and lay it at His feet. When we're honest about our loneliness and allow Him in, He begins to fill those empty spaces and breathe new life into our situation. Whether I am in a crowd of people, or isolated in my house, I have Someone who will never leave me or forsake me. You do, too. It's a promise I am trusting in, for myself and for all my dear friends who are walking through broken places. I keep breathing in the name of *Jesus* – a reminder that I am never alone.

Love Lessons

Songs from a Bronx Basement

Our music ministry tour was halfway through when I ended up in a basement to help with an emergency. We were ministering in a rough part of Bronx, New York, and as we started our afternoon of work, the staff director led me down to the food pantry for the homeless.

"She's been beaten again, this time with a baseball bat," the director said as I stared at a young woman lying in a fetal position on the floor. She was bloody, with bruises across her face and arms, and her hair was patchy. A few of her fingernails were missing.

"We don't know if she's going to make it," the staff director told me. "The ambulance may not even come because this happens so often. Can you stay with her until we can get her some help?"

A thought ran through my head: *Why was I the one chosen?* But I quickly reminded myself we had a purpose here, and God was in control of everything we encountered. This was beyond what I had expected, so I reminded God that I really needed Him, like right now! "You there, God? Because I can't do *this*. Not in my strength." I prayed and felt a momentary rush of calm. One lone rocking chair sat in a corner of the basement, so I gathered the young woman in my arms and pulled her onto my lap. The chair creaked as we rocked back and forth, and I wondered when help would come. The woman didn't seem to be conscious, but I did the only thing that made sense in the moment. I started singing.

At one point, her body was so still that I feared she had passed away, until one finger moved. I kept rocking, singing, praying, and trusting that if I loved her with all my heart, she would feel that love. I kept singing songs my mom and grandma would sing over me when I was hurting, and songs from our tour concerts. I sang about heaven and healing, and felt God's presence stronger than ever.

Her name was Sarah. She didn't have a home, and I didn't know if she had family. It was obvious there were people in Sarah's life who brought her harm, abusing her body and mind. But she mattered to God, and He was holding her in His arms – only that afternoon His arms were mine. In a creaky rocking chair, He used me to communicate His love for her.

After singing all the songs I knew by heart, my voice was wearing thin. I stopped for a few minutes and saw Sarah's eyelashes flutter. Her body felt a little warmer than when we first began rocking in the chair and I was hopeful. I began to pray aloud, asking God to heal her and remind her that she had great purpose. I sobbed as I prayed, crying out to God in desperation. She reached over and grabbed my finger and gave it a gentle squeeze, as if she was holding on with the little strength she had left. I started singing again through my tears.

I missed the concert that night because I sang to an audience of one – in the basement of a building in the Bronx, holding this woman whose life was so different from mine. Her eyes finally opened, and they were a deep blue, with red broken blood vessels surrounding them. She smiled, and despite missing most of her teeth, it was a beautiful sight.

By the time a paramedic arrived, Sarah was sitting up and drinking from a water bottle one of the ministry staff brought us. The paramedic looked shocked, and I wondered if he had expected to pick up a lifeless body.

The next day, I learned that a precious family in the church we were partnering with paid for Sarah's medical bills and made a place for her in their home, harboring her from the dangerous people in her life. The family knew God had plans for Sarah. Before we left for our next stop, the family told me Sarah remembered the woman who sang in the basement rocking chair with her, and the songs touched her in a way that made her curious. She wanted to know what the lady in the rocking chair had, and whatever it was, she wanted it, too. The family prayed with her, and that day she began a new journey. I lost touch with the family after a few years, but the last time we talked, I learned Sarah was regaining her health and involved in a support group for battered women that met at the church. And Sarah had discovered she loved to sing. In fact, she began singing in the church choir, and felt like she found purpose. Singing brought her joy and peace.

Sarah changed my life that afternoon. We spent time in a sacred space – a basement – and we each found that God's strong arms hold us up, give us a song, and bring new purpose in the most surprising ways.

Words That Heal

"Sticks and stones may break my bones, but words will never hurt me."

I heard a little boy chant these words, then run away in tears as I passed the school playground on my daily walking route. Some things never change. I remember hearing those exact words in elementary school, but now I can't make sense of them. Let's not kid ourselves, words have power. God spoke the galaxies into existence with words (Genesis 1:3). On a human level, our words also have power. They transfer ideas, heal, educate, and bring laughter. But they can also hurt us in deep places. My husband says it takes a hundred "atta boys!" to overcome a hurtful comment. I agree.

A recent coffee date with a dear friend showed me the power of words. She had been hurt by gossip, and the careless, ugly comments had broken her. "It's so hard to not react out of hurt," said my friend. "I will take time and respond in love, but, boy, that can be tough, right?"

Yes, it can! As I looked at her situation from the outside, it was apparent the person who hurt her spoke out of jealousy. My friend is one of the most beautiful, giving, Godly leaders I know, and the hurt she experienced came out of nowhere. She was trying to walk through it in love, and not return hurtful words, but instead give life and light.

Words can wound and steal life. Gossip and slander bring a short, cheap thrill that can leave lasting scars. But there are also healing words (Proverbs 12:18). Words of encouragement give courage to those who are weak, afraid, and torn down. *A gentle answer turns away wrath* (Proverbs 15:1).

Luke 6:45 is worth meditating on as we think about the power of words: *For out of the overflow of his heart, his mouth speaks.* Our words become healing as we replace the negativity in our hearts. At some point in our lives, we have all been hurt by words, probably more than we can count. I have. Damaging words can make us doubt our worth and cause us to feel alone. But encouraging words are like a breath of fresh air, moving us forward in positive directions.

I am intentional about speaking positive words over people in my prayers for them. I speak scripture, the Father's benediction, and bathe my thoughts of them with words like "you are special, you are beautiful, you are loved." The positive words I pray drown out the negative judgments of the outside world. They are beloved. Words matter.

I read in one of my devotionals that "for us to gain the Father's benediction, Jesus had to lose it." At his baptism, Jesus received the good word from on high. On the cross, He heard no word from the Father, only deafening silence. The silence did not break Jesus's bones like sticks and stones, but it broke every other part of Him. It was for our healing. Heaven's silence toward Jesus secured the Father's "good word" toward us once and for all. The beauty of that truth should melt our hearts and transform our words, giving us the desire to speak healing and love to everyone we meet.

The Elevator Hug

As we descended in the elevator, the little girl beside me whispered to her mother, straining to keep her voice low, but we were crammed close together and everyone heard her.

"Mommy, I think that lady needs a hug."

The little girl was talking about me, and she was right. I had just left the doctor's office after several tests and lots of "what next" questions without answers. My mood was reflected in my face, which the little girl had been staring at since we walked on the elevator together. Her blue eyes looked up at me with concern.

The mother shook her head and told the little girl not to bother me.

After a few seconds, she tugged on her mother's skirt and, again, whispered loudly. "Can I *please* give that lady a hug?"

Before her mother could tell her no again, I said I would love a hug and knelt. She grabbed my neck so hard I had to catch my breath. This gave bear hugs a new meaning, but I didn't mind. The little girl knew a hug was what I needed at that moment, and nothing was going to stop her.

I couldn't quit thinking about that little girl's determination to make someone's day a little brighter, and for the next few days, I paid closer attention to the people around me. It seems like so many of us go through the day struggling to find joy, like me on the elevator that day. They are buried in worries, or feel unappreciated, and sometimes wonder if they have a purpose. The more I looked around, the more convinced I became that we need more people like the little elevator girl. So, I did an experiment over the next few months. Some people call it "pay it forward," others call it "random acts of kindness," or "planting seeds." The labels didn't matter to me; I just wanted to tell others they mattered, and someone cared. How many people go through the day without hearing a kind word or seeing a smile? I suspected too many, so I got intentional about my experiment. I prayed God would show me people who needed a random act of kindness, and He answered my prayers.

It started with helping my elderly neighbor take out her trash during the week and expanded to nursing home visits. I went down the halls and gave free hugs in honor of my little elevator friend. My dog, Holly, came with me, and the residents adored her. I listened to their stories and asked questions, eager to learn what made these people who they are today. One man thanked me for taking the time to hear his story.

"Nobody ever listens to me anymore," he said, his eyes brighter than when I first sat down with him. I imagined he felt like me after my elevator hug. Someone took the time to communicate that he mattered. As Holly and I walked out the door, I turned back around to see a small crowd of residents waving goodbye, asking when I would come back. "Soon," I told them.

My next adventure was handing out water and Gatorade to the construction workers stuck in the summer heat. I had passed the workers and said a prayer of thanks for them, but God nudged me to do a little more. I popped into a nearby grocery store and bought the drinks, then passed them out. "What you are doing matters," I said to each person. They all seemed caught off guard, and I think the cold drinks and my words of appreciation did more for me than them. I felt God's presence in amazing ways, and my worries faded. Go figure!

A few weeks later, my daughter and I were shopping for a desk and found one, but we couldn't reach the box on a high shelf. A nearby store employee looked like he wanted to be anywhere else that day.

"Mom, I don't think we should bother him," my daughter said. "He's not happy."

The sign on the shelf instructed us to ask an employee to pull boxes from the shelves, so I requested his help. He practically groaned when I opened my mouth to speak, and then grumbled the entire time he was retrieving the box.

"Sir, thank you for what you do," I said after he put the desk in our cart. "I appreciate you."

He looked at me suspiciously.

"I just wanted you to know what you do matters," I said.

"You're the first person in months to thank me." He walked with us to the checkout and told me the story of a lady who had just finished yelling at him because the lamp she wanted was out of stock. By the time we got to the front of the store, the three of us were laughing. After he loaded the desk into our car, the store employee shook my hand and said, "Thank you for helping me remember to laugh."

I've found that random acts of kindness require intentionality at the start of our day. God honors our prayers when we ask Him to put people in our path who need the kindness we can freely give.

I hope I see that little elevator girl again someday, because it's my turn to give her a big hug. She has no idea her compassion helped me begin a journey of paying it forward to others. The day before I wrote this, I was in the drive-through at Starbucks when I realized my purse was at home. I scrounged for change in my car but couldn't come up with enough to pay for my coffee. When I got to the window, ready to explain my predicament, the woman smiled.

"No worries. The man ahead of you paid for your coffee."

That moment felt like another hug on an elevator, and I thanked God for random acts of kindness. Now, I'm off to pay it forward.

A Teddy Bear Perspective

Some days feel like a gut punch. This was one of those days. It seemed as if bad news was lurking around every corner, and I shuddered at the thought of answering the phone. The week had been one of loss – five dear friends, and one who had battled the same cancer as Mom. She had helped me deliver care packages to chemo patients, never complaining or wavering, always encouraging and blessing others. She had the same spirit as Mom's: "Let's put our party hats on and do this." I missed her and was grieving.

I walked out of an appointment with a heavy heart and breathed a prayer. There were no words to express how dark things felt. "Lord, please just help." A simple prayer, but sometimes those reach God's heart deeper than the wordy, eloquent ones. I said my "amen" and then noticed an elderly gentleman in a wheelchair. He was being taken to his appointment and behind him, a mother and her young daughter were walking hand in hand. The little girl was carrying a stuffed bear in one arm, and I walked behind them for a short distance before the girl let go of her mother's hand and ran to the elderly man. She reached out and gave him the stuffed bear, then hurried back with a wide smile and grabbed her mother's hand again.

The man went into his appointment with that bear wrapped in his arms and a tear in his eye.

I caught up with the woman and learned that she had recently lost her father to COVID. The little girl had adored her grandpa and felt the loss deeply. He was her best friend, and the man in the wheelchair reminded the little girl of him. Still clutching her mother's hand, she looked up at me and said, "He will be okay now. He's got a bear."

I walked to my car with tears blurring my eyes. This beautiful display of kindness touched my soul, an answer to my not-so-eloquent prayer. In the simple act of a child, God had given me a picture of all that was good in the world. I decided from that moment forward I would look around to see it. I wanted to notice goodness and allow it to keep changing my perspective. Yes, there is bad in the world, but I don't have to make that my focus. All those little, positive moments are big things. As I looked around with my heart and eyes, it was amazing what I noticed:

- My friend spending the afternoon with someone who was suffering from Alzheimer's.
- Volunteers packing hundreds of bags that were going to bless cancer patients.
- Sweet 97-year-old Anna working on her prayer quilt, and the other angels beside her who give tirelessly as they create quilted blessings for others.
- My neighbor mowing the grass for a lady who lost her husband.

I sat on my porch swing and looked at the blue sky and listened to the traffic behind us (which we usually complain about) feeling thankful for breath, my dogs, and another day. I decided the traffic sounds didn't matter anymore. That little girl had changed my perspective. No matter how many trials we endure or how dark the world seems, there is always good to be found. Genuine people are all around us, giving, serving, and blessing. Most of the time, like the little girl, they are doing good behind the scenes, but they are making a big difference. The world is a better place because of them.

The heaviness lifted and I embraced the quiet. Focusing on the good in the world chipped away at the insignificant, and what emerged were small things that add up to so much good. I allowed myself to sink back into the shelter of the Most High and feel safe in the shadow of the Almighty (Psalm 91).

Are you weary, tired, burdened, or fearful? Are you faltering under those gut punches the world delivers? Take some time to look around and change your perspective. Good moments are happening all around you, and God wants you to notice them. I pray we can all be like this little girl. During her pain, she reached out in kindness to someone who was right in front of her. She changed his perspective, and she changed mine. It was a small act, but it had a huge impact. Love is like that. It finds us on a day that seems small and dark, then opens us to the wide paths of light. Let's walk in that light and look for the arms that are reaching out to share good in the world.

Dressing Room Cries

I heard the sobs coming from the dressing room beside me and wondered if I should call for help. They were gut-wrenching sounds, and then I heard her words.

"I'm too fat, too fat."

The woman in the room next to mine had slid to the floor, and I could picture her leaning up against the mirror, unable to look at herself any longer. "How did this happen?" The sobs continued, and after a few minutes, she stood back up. I could hear zipping and tugging.

"I'm going to be the ugliest one there," she said through her sobs.

I had an armload of dresses of my own to try on, and as I began the process, my heart went out to the woman. Dressing rooms are no fun. As a young woman, I hated my body. That feeling of "too fat" followed me every time I had to buy new clothes, look at myself in the mirror, walk into a crowded room. I remember that panicky feeling in the dressing room, wishing for a different body and comparing myself to a standard I could never live up to. It was a journey to learn how to love myself just as God created me, but some days I still struggle with this.

That afternoon in the dressing room, I had just come from

meeting with one of my dearest friends to discuss her latter stage cancer prognosis. I had been in tears most of the morning and wanted to get the dress shopping over with. I hate shopping, but the time with my friend had put things in perspective.

Hearing those sobs next door made me wish I could take the woman in my arms and tell her she was worth so much more than what she looked like on the outside. She continued to groan, tug, zip, and mutter under her breath. I exited the dressing room with my rejects and shopped for a while longer. By the time I had loaded up with more dresses to try on, the woman was sitting outside the dressing rooms in a chair beside her husband, empty-handed and eyes red from crying.

I tried on a few more dresses and walked out with my final choice, then hung it on the rack by the cashier.

"I love that dress," the woman from the dressing room said, and I thanked her.

"Did you find something?" I asked, and she shook her head.

"There's nothing for me here."

She sat for a minute, looking at the dress while the cashier rang up my purchase.

"Is your dress for a special occasion?" she asked, and I told her it was for an event related to my therapy dogs. Her eyes lit up, and I showed her a picture of my dogs. She and her husband had just lost their dog, and we talked about how that feeling of loss lingers. We had an instant connection, and I decided to ask if I could help her find a dress.

"I bet there is one here just for you," I said.

She glanced at her husband and then shook her head again. "There's nothing here for me."

I smiled. "Let's just look."

We walked around the racks for about 15 minutes, picking out styles of dresses that would complement her figure. I talked about visiting my friend that morning and told the woman I had also been dreading dress shopping. The only way I could get through it, I said, was to start listing things I was thankful for. "I bet you could name five things you're grateful for," I said to her as she looked into the three-way mirror outside the dressing room. The dress she wore was a fit, and she smiled and quickly named five things.

There are voices in our head that tell us we don't measure up. We say negative things to ourselves every day and listen to the noise about who we should be and what we should look like. We see images that warp the view we have of ourselves, causing us to believe we're not enough if we're not perfect.

The woman's sobs were the cries of so many who feel unworthy when they look at themselves in the mirror. It's a broken place and walking out of it isn't easy. Gratitude and perspective help, but so does hearing that we all struggle with society's expectations. When we speak authentically to one another about our worth, it drowns out the noise and allows us to look in the mirror and see the true beauty looking back at us.

Desert Encounters

My parking space that day was far away from the hospital, and it was cold, even in the hospital's covered garage. I grumbled under my breath about that crummy parking space as I hurried with my hands shoved into my pockets and my ears turning blue. When I finished my visit, it was a long elevator ride back to the garage and my car. My time in the hospital had been a hard couple of hours. It was another goodbye I wasn't ready for, so I closed my eyes and leaned my head back to breathe in the name of Jesus. A woman was the only other person with me in the elevator, and I could hear her gasping, as if she was trying to catch her breath. I opened my eyes, and she lowered her mask to say something, but words didn't come – only an audible moan as her eyes filled with tears.

I wasn't sure what to do, so I reached out my hand toward her. Without hesitation, she grabbed it and squeezed hard, then I quietly repeated the name of Jesus, this time in a whisper so she could hear. It was a prayer of sorts; except I didn't know what to pray for. There was nothing I could say to ease her pain, but I felt God's powerful presence in that elevator. His arms were wrapped around us both, so I whispered the name of Jesus again. She finally said two words: "He's gone."

I don't know who "he" was, or what the situation had been, but it was clear the loss had shattered her. Leaving her at this moment wasn't an option, so I walked with the woman until she found her car. Which, as it turned out, happened to be right next to mine. Remember that parking space I was grumbling about? I sure remembered, and then reminded myself that nothing is an accident.

She opened her door and turned to hug me. As she sat down, she looked at me and pulled down her mask. "Thank you," she said. Her voice was shaky and filled with pain. "You pray, don't you?"

"I sure do," I replied.

"Can you please pray for me and my family?"

In that cold parking garage, we prayed together. I didn't know what she had walked through, but I was certain God was with her, and I told her this as I finished our prayer.

She smiled. "I asked God where He was in all this pain. And He showed me today in that elevator. Thank you for being here. You don't know me, but you took the time to help me today."

Since I was parked beside her, and because I had Resilience Care Boxes in my trunk (again, there are no accidents), I put a box in her car. As she pulled out of the parking spot, she smiled again, tears running down her cheeks. She mouthed the words, "Thank you," and drove away.

I started my car and sat for a moment, trying to wrap my head around what had just happened. Every morning, I pray, "Lord, let nothing in my day be an accident." And once again, He showed me even the toughest moments and heartbreaking goodbyes can have His handprints all over them. My devotional that day was about the desert, and today felt like one of those dry places where everything seems a little desolate. Another loss for both me and my elevator friend had left us parched. And yet, God was there, orchestrating events so she and I could meet in that desert. There is a divine dialogue in these dry places. We don't need introductions or explanations. Groans and simple prayers can bring hurting souls together for comfort. She needed me, and I needed her.

I may never meet that lady again, but in the elevator our pain collided, and it was no accident. God wrapped His arms around us both, and it was a sacred moment of beauty in the desert.

Are You the Gift?

It is early morning and I notice her again. She is in a hurry, ringing a doorbell, carefully placing a box on a porch, and then rushing to the next house. I don't know her name, so I call her the "nice delivery lady" when I talk about her. On my daily prayer walks I watch her driving by, and then I wave and say a prayer for the "nice delivery lady." I'm led to pray for her, not knowing what the needs might be, but confident there is something in her life that isn't perfect, a small piece of brokenness that might weigh her heart down on certain days.

This week while I was walking, she ran back from delivering a package and stopped before getting in her van. "Hi! I see you walking and talking to yourself every day!"

I laughed and replied, "Well, I am actually on my prayer walk, and praying. But I probably look like I'm having a long conversation with myself!" I told her that I whispered a prayer for her every time I saw her truck. Her eyes filled with tears, and she looked shocked. "Me? You pray for *me*?"

I told her it made me happy to watch her wave to the security cameras on front porches and notice the spring in her step. I wanted her to know I appreciated her faithfulness and joy as she made those deliveries. "God sees it too!" I said. "Keep up the great work because people notice. What you do matters!"

Her tears kept coming and she replied, "I think your prayers have kept me going these past few months. Please keep praying for me." Her voice was sincere, and she added, "Oh, *please* keep praying." She didn't tell me her story, but she didn't need to. There was a reason God prompted me to pray for my delivery friend, and I assured her the prayers would continue. She wiped her tears and waved. Her smile was back and off she went.

I thanked God for the privilege of praying for her. I don't know who she is, but her story and her purpose matter. And she matters to God more than she could imagine. So, I will keep my promise and continue to pray for the "nice delivery lady."

These days, I pay close attention when God prompts me to pray. He puts someone on my heart I pass during the day, and He whispers: *Pray for her. Pray for him.* I don't ignore those whispers. In fact, I listen for them. Even on days when my life throws challenges and hurdles at me, I pray when prompted and it always lifts my spirits. Prayer changes things, including me.

My favorite author, Ann Voskamp says, "Be the gift." We can be a gift to those who we may never meet, offering them the smallest bit of joy, taking the time to weep with them, or gently promising they will be in our prayers. When we are the gift, we receive the gift. The greatest blessings in my life have come when I made the choice to serve others. Serving heals and brings hope to a weary soul, and there are many out there. Sometimes it's just taking the time to slow down and notice. My encouragement for you today is to "Be the gift" to someone. Amazing things happen from small acts, so pay attention to those moments when you feel God prompting you. Your act of service can change someone, and it might change you too.

Be the gift. It turns your brokenness into abundance!

Holly and Emily

Emily was determined to run around the track with her classmates, but her crutches slowed her down. Holly, my therapy dog, and I were helping with a special needs gym class, although the moment I walked into the room, it was obvious the label underestimated these kids. They were the most "able" children I've ever met – strong, determined, and with smiles that were authentic, despite the challenges they faced every day.

I watched as Emily struggled to make it around the track, hobbling alone but smiling. This was a moment for Holly, so I walked over to her and asked if my dog could walk with her. It only took her a few minutes to warm up to Holly, and before long she was moving a little faster around the track with the extra support. A few times, Emily stopped and wrapped her arms around Holly, then kissed her on the head. It was heaven for both – Holly getting love, and Emily with a faithful companion at her side. My therapy dog was working hard and loving every minute. This is what we trained her to do, and she did it with patience and grace.

The teacher told me it was the first time Emily had made it around the entire track, and I was proud of Holly and this precious little girl. After they finished the loop, Emily grabbed my hand.

"Miss Lisa, did you know that Holly loves Jesus?"

I nodded. "She sure does!"

Emily thought for a few minutes and looked back up at me.

"And you love Jesus, too. Want to know how I know?"

I nodded, holding back tears.

"I see your hearts, and there's sunshine in there because that's where Jesus lives. I love Jesus, too. He makes me happy every day."

I couldn't have come up with a simpler way to express my faith. Jesus lives in me, and His love brings light that spreads out from me to others. But it was Emily's light that changed my day. She had no idea how deeply she blessed my heart as I watched her connection with Holly, and the trust she put in my dog. She wasn't afraid to accept that she needed some help to make it around, and during the journey, she found joy.

The teacher told me that Emily's disability hinders her physically, but that she lights up the room every time she walks in. She may not walk like other children, but it doesn't matter to Emily.

On the way home, I looked over at Holly, who seemed to grin at me from the passenger's seat. My encounter with Emily felt like warm sunshine, just like she had talked about. We can either focus on our negative situation and force everyone else around us to endure our pessimism, or we can choose to spread sunshine. It sounds so simple, but it rarely is. I let a thousand things take away that light every day. I get caught up in drama and let it drag me down into the muck of strife and sadness. Or little things get under my skin, and I grumble and complain. Emily showed me a different way. Lean on Jesus, walk in the sunshine, and be grateful for the journey.

Cancer Journey

Hair Raising

My father shaved my mother's head on Easter, after the chemo treatments had taken their toll on her beautiful hair. "Jesus rose today," Mom said. "And my hair will, too."

She loved her dark hair and had always hurried to the salon as soon as she saw the first gray roots returning. She couldn't stand the thought of going gray, even though I told her many times that her hair would look beautiful in its natural state. I ached for her when the very last strands of her hair were gone. It was the physical manifestation of what was taking place in her body, a discouraging reminder of what cancer takes from us. Having her head shaved was difficult, but she never looked back or complained about what was ahead.

A year later, as I was driving Mom to her hair appointment, I looked over at her full head of beautiful gray hair. Her hair had been "raised" again, and she looked better than ever. It had grown back thicker and frosty white. There was no more covering the gray. It was there for all the world to see, and Mom couldn't have been happier to look in the mirror.

"If I could write," she told me, "I would write about my hair, and how it shows me that God cares about the little things. He gave me a heavenly frost."

I'm writing this for her because I want to remember how God was with us through every step of the journey. Through losing her hair, God reminded Mom that even the little things were in His line of vision. Hair. It would have been easy to miss this detail if we had been focused on all the troubles that surrounded us. God is always working the details out in His timing to remind us how much He loves us. *Indeed, the very hairs of your head are all numbered. Don't be afraid; you are worth more than many sparrows* (Luke 12:7). God knew everything about Mom, even down to the number of hairs on her head, and how hard it would be for her when they were gone.

When the stylist had finished and we were about to walk out of the salon, she winked at Mom. "Do you know how many people would pay good money to have your hair color?"

Mom and I smiled at each other. She had never seemed more happy or active in her life than during the days she was walking with God on the cancer journey. She talked about those little details because she was noticing them more than ever before. I took her wise words to heart and applied them to my own situation. In my discouragement about my health challenges, God had been beside me every second – protecting me, putting me in the right place at the right time, leading me to doctors who could diagnose, treat, and perform surgery, and providing little financial miracles along the way. We often overlook what we've been given in a difficult situation because we're too focused on wishing the situation would go away. But God sends us answers to the small details if we pay attention.

God's miracles are sometimes *not* answering our prayers because He knows a better way. On my worst days, it's a sure bet that if I'm feeling discouraged, it's because I'm staring at the wrong things.

During the days when Mom and I were sitting through chemo

treatments and doctor visits, her joy permeated everything. It's what I still remember. And during that time, we laughed, cried, and prayed harder than ever, knowing that whatever happens, God is there for it all – big or small.

He doesn't waste any of our experiences, even the ones we'd rather leave behind. God gave Mom what He promised. For the rest of her journey, she had the most beautiful head of hair, and it gave her joy. But the greater joy was knowing she was never alone, and that God would walk beside her to the end of that journey. He paid attention to every detail along the way, and Mom followed His lead.

The Choice

I gave Mom a big kiss as an orderly wheeled her into surgery. She and I had agreed that no matter what the results were, everything would be okay. I watched her go and wondered if I would feel that way if the results sent us further down the path of more treatments and uncertainty. Cancer is a winding road that doesn't always include signs to tell us what comes next.

The waiting room was busy, and a tall, frail-looking man sat down beside me. His hands were trembling as he thrust one out and introduced himself as Bob. During the two hours we sat next to one another, Bob talked to me about the wife he loved and the life they enjoyed together. Now she was ill, and his full-time job was caring for her. Even though her illness had ended the traveling and the adventures they had enjoyed together, he had no complaints. Then Bob said something that changed my perspective. "In life, we get to make a choice. Be happy or be miserable. I choose happy."

Bob and his wife had been married 60 years, and when he talked about her, his eyes sparkled. But then, he would tear up and his chin would tremble when he contemplated losing her. He would miss the love of his life, but the choice was clear. He would be happy through it all. "When I can't feel that happiness, because my human heart is broken, God will choose it for me."

When Bob's wife was out of surgery, he hurried from the waiting room with a quick wave. I told him I would pray for him. That night, as I was leaving the hospital, I saw Bob leaning over the bed railing in his wife's room as he kissed her hands and stroked her face. He was smiling, and in that moment, I knew Bob meant every word he said to me in the waiting room. I don't know the outcome of her surgery, but Bob was choosing happy no matter what.

As I drove home, my heart was full, and my mind was churning with thoughts about my conversation with Bob. He had radiated not only happiness, but a deep love for his wife and God. Bob had placed her in God's hands and was walking forward from that place of trust. When we encounter someone who radiates love, it stays with us for a while. I thought about difficult times during Mom's cancer journey when I had made the conscious decision to be happy despite all the reasons to be depressed. During those bleak days, choosing happiness brought me strength, and I could feel God pouring out His grace. *Yes, God, I will accept this less-than-perfect place I am in, and delight in you. I choose happiness because of your great love for me.*

It's easy to believe we'll always choose to be happy, but sometimes when the circumstances are draining and we can't see what's ahead, happiness can seem like a foolish option. And if we dig our heels in and determine that we will choose happiness, the enemy will try to divert us with worries and fears. Another pops up as soon as we've whacked one down. It's just as Bob said: a choice. Choosing happy is powerful and goes against everything that makes sense. Why would we choose happiness when there is so much to worry and complain about? Isn't it easier to give in?

When we choose to smile instead of frown, to send a positive message instead of a panicked cry, we are sharing with the world – and ourselves – that we trust God to keep His promises.

I discovered that allowing the clouds of negativity to weigh me down blocks what God wants to do in my life. I can't see the possibilities when I'm covered in darkness. Even in the painful times, we can choose the kind of happiness that lasts. One of my favorite quotes is, "When you change the way you look at things, the things you look at change."

Find the arms of Jesus and the happy place that only He can provide. It's the place that leads to freedom and miracles you never dreamed possible.

Broken Nails and Bad Coffee

I was standing in line for an iced tea at the coffee shop when I heard a distressed voice behind me. A lady was lamenting over the poor quality of the coffee, and she didn't seem to mind if everyone around her knew it. I was grabbing a drink before spending the day with Mom. She and I weren't going to the mall, doing lunch, or – like the lady and her daughter behind me – enjoying a coffee date. Instead, we would spend the day near our favorite window in the chemo treatment room, while Mom endured another round of what we hoped would fight off the cancer cells in her body.

The lady behind me then gasped about her broken nail. She was furious about it and used a few expletives to communicate to her daughter what a crummy day she was having. I thought maybe a smile would help, so I turned my head. The daughter's expression was tense, and I could tell she wasn't enjoying her mother's rant any more than the rest of us.

"Do you know how I feel?" the mother said to me when I smiled at her. Her question surprised me, and I thought about how to respond. Yes, I did understand how she felt. A thousand times I had complained about this or that aggravating detail (perhaps not so loudly, however). I had grumbled about a moment gone wrong in my day or felt annoyed by inconveniences that threw my schedule off. But these days, I had become aware of how often I make insignificant details loom large. How many times had I forgotten that life gives us far more good moments than bad ones?

The lady continued to stare at me, waiting for my response. She wanted someone to share her disappointment, and her daughter stood silently.

"Yes, I know how you feel," I replied, and she looked satisfied. I told her I was getting tea to go, so I could accompany my mom to her chemo treatment.

She looked surprised and asked what kind of cancer, and we began to talk. The lady's name was Bridget, and by the time it was my turn to order, I had told her all about Mom, our journey, and how much we looked forward to time together on chemo treatment days. "It's not the most exciting way to spend the day," I said, "but I want to grab every second I can with my mom. Things have a way of changing fast."

Bridget apologized to both me and her daughter for her outburst, and I told her no apology was necessary. After all, I ordered the tea instead of the coffee. We laughed and continued to talk as she and her daughter placed their order.

"Actually," she said, "the coffee here isn't *so* terrible."

Her daughter's face seemed relieved, and Bridget continued. "And you know, superglue will take care of this nail." She held up her finger with the broken nail and winked at me.

A few years ago, I might have been the person who thought bad coffee and a broken nail could ruin my day, but perspectives change when we're faced with the fragility of life. It's a precious gift we've been given. On the way to my car, I thought about Mom sitting in that chemo chair, cheerily facing another day of uncertainty. During our journey, Jesus was closer than ever, reminding me the things that matter in life aren't things at all.

I picked up Mom for treatment, and we found our favorite recliner – the one under the window so we could feel the sunshine and see the sky. We laughed a lot that day. Someone who didn't know us might think we didn't have a care in the world, but we knew better. We were celebrating another day, another hour, another minute. There was so much to be thankful for, and we were determined to squeeze everything out of this day. I want to remember all the lessons this journey has taught me. Bad coffee? I'll take it. Broken nail? Find the superglue. We're all going to be okay.

A Beauty Day

We gave Mom a gift certificate one Christmas for a full day of pampering at a local salon. She would enjoy a facial, makeover, haircut, and style. When the day came, I accompanied her to the salon, and tears streamed down my cheeks as I watched the stylist blow dry her hair. I remembered back to the day Dad shaved it all off, and now here we were, with hair to spare!

We went to lunch after her day of pampering, and Mom was radiant. I wanted to etch that image in my mind so I would never forget how beautiful she was, even during the hardest battle of her life. Mom always believed that no matter how bad the day is, or how dark our life may look, there is always something good to hang onto. Sometimes, when we're desperate to find that positive place, we look for something big and grand. But most of the time, it's the little things that get us through the day. A smile. Encouraging words from a friend. A thank you note in the mail. A haircut and style.

When we notice the good, we should grab it, and God will take it from there. At lunch that day, Mom reminded me that miracles can blossom from a very tiny, good thing. As she walked through each day of her journey, Mom lived what she believed. She looked around for the things we often miss and clutched them tightly. She was thankful for so many things I missed.

That day in the salon, she embraced every moment. When I looked around, I wondered if for most people, this was just another task to be checked off the list. Grocery store. Post office. Salon. Dry Cleaners. Pick up kids. But for Mom, this was a gift, and not just because it had come to her in a fancy Christmas envelope. She was savoring every moment, soaking in all the seemingly trivial things that took place. The washing, drying, cutting, styling. It wasn't just another day at the salon for her. You could see from her expression that every moment mattered.

She accepted our gift graciously, but it felt like I also received a gift that day. It was the best Christmas gift I've ever given or received. Watching Mom grab onto the good in everything is a priceless treasure that I carry with me. When she walked out of that salon, it was not only the makeover and hairstyle that made her beautiful, but she radiated inner joy. She focused on the good and was grateful for it.

I'm doing my best to walk through hard days with this same attitude – opening my eyes to what is around me, grabbing the good, and holding onto it. It's a legacy Mom left me, and one that I want to pass on. I'll warn you: it isn't easy. Our human nature is to focus on the negative and miss those small blessings. I'm getting there. I had an excellent teacher.

Grief, Thanksgiving, and Ducks

Eight years ago, on Thanksgiving Day, I knelt to tie Mom's shoe and could see something wasn't right. She looked at me with a blank stare and no words, her eyes trying to communicate what I already knew. The blank stare was a series of strokes that led to her homegoing a few weeks later. I remember trying to act normal that day, as if my world wasn't falling apart. I helped Mom eat her last Thanksgiving meal, my heart breaking as I lifted the fork to her mouth.

How do we fold our hands in a prayer of thanks when our hearts are broken? A friend and I visited recently about the loss of her child during this season, a pain I can't comprehend. I watched her walk through that pain, and there are no words to describe it.

"They say time heals," she said, tears spilling down her cheeks, "but I'm not too sure about that." The beautiful season of Thanksgiving was also making her relive the raw grief of loss. There are many of us who face the holidays with painful memories and others who are struggling through the middle of a broken place. It's hard to lift your hands in praise when your heart is crushed.

I started a gratitude journal when Mom's cancer and my

autoimmune journeys began. She told me I would find healing when I found gratitude in everyday moments. That journal pulled me out of grief and shifted my focus on what was in front of me, not what was beyond my reach. There are so many things we can't control, but we *can* choose gratitude. At first, I didn't think it was possible to write one word. The journeys we were on left me feeling dark and alone. But I knew Mom was right, so I wrote my thanks every day. After she died, I felt like putting the journal away, but instead I took it with me to the porch swing where we had shared so many conversations and tears. There would be no more time on the swing with Mom, and I sat with pen in hand and journal in my lap and let tears fall on the page. After a while, I wrote one word.

Duck.

The ducks Mom and I used to watch were huddled together by their pond for warmth, and I was thankful for them. I let myself grieve the loss of my mother, tears falling as I watched those ducks. And then, I felt my own warmth grow as peace blanketed me. That single word was all I needed in my journal that day. It was a reminder of all that I had to be thankful for. Just as the ducks were hovering for warmth from the cold, I needed peace and warmth, too. Jesus met me there and sheltered me. He allowed me to be honest about my grief, and He held me close.

When my friend's child was dying in the hospital during that Thanksgiving season, God also met her during those moments of helplessness. "He showered me with indescribable peace," she said. She was also choosing to find moments of gratitude during the Thanksgiving season, even though it was hard. She wanted the memories of loss to be covered with hope, but some days that choice to be grateful was easier than others.

Ann Voskamp talks about our broken hearts being "re-membered." This happens when we defy the dark and see the goodness of a good and holy God. When we have seen, and know, the face of God and His kindness, our hands will raise in thanksgiving.

If you are walking through grief and a broken place, my prayer is that you will feel carried and know the peace that passes all understanding. As you hover for relief from the cold pain, I pray that you are "re-membered" through His grace.

You are never alone.

The Man in Mom's Chair

The man glanced at my shirt, and his words flew toward me in a rage. "Ministry, huh?" he growled. "I don't believe in God, so your ministry doesn't need to waste time on me." He told me he was dying of cancer, and he asked me where God had been. "People don't care, so don't bother praying for me."

I sat down beside him to listen as he poured out anger, sadness, and fear. I heard the hurt in his soul, and I understood because I've felt that same hurt. In fact, pain was the genesis for the nonprofit Mom began, and then Lisa Bain Ministries as we carry forward her legacy. We sit beside people as they go through dark tunnels, offering our time and small gifts of hope.

I was silent after the man finished sharing his pain, then I reached over and pulled a handmade prayer quilt across his legs. His hands were shaking from the cold, and he refused to make eye contact.

"Are you hungry?" I asked.

"In fact, I am," he said, still looking away.

I handed him a snack bag from one of our Resilience Care Boxes. "I have just what you need, and even something that might help with the nausea."

His head turned toward me, and his eyes narrowed.

"What do you know about nausea?"

I told him I had sat in this same chair years ago when Mom would grab peppermints to settle her stomach. "We walked through cancer together, which is why I'm here today. In fact, that chair you are in was her favorite chemo chair because it was near the window, and we always needed a little brightness when we were here." I told him I was remembering a conversation with Mom, as she sat in the same chair he was now in.

"Really?" he said, his eyes softening. "What was it about?"

"It was raining, and we watched the drops gather on the window glass and listened to the soothing sound. My mom talked about how our difficult journey made the raindrops beautiful and spring colors more vibrant. The rain was helping her flowers grow and bloom, and it was all good. Mom was thankful for the rain that day. It eased her soul."

He pulled the quilt up and waited to hear if there was more to the story.

"The cancer was getting the upper hand, and as we left that day, I grabbed my umbrella to keep her dry, but she waved it off and told me 'Not today.' She wanted to feel the rain on her face while she still could. When we got in the car, we were completely soaked, and we laughed. 'There goes my good hair day,' Mom said. And you know, she was bald from the chemo."

I saw the man's lips almost curve into an understanding smile.

"Our view of rain changed throughout her cancer journey. I don't think you ever go through something hard without it changing you – either for the good or the bad. My mom chose to make the journey count for good, which is why I'm sitting here with you today."

I finished my story and pulled out a stuffed Mabel Joy pup from the box and put it in his arms. I laid a gas card on top of the stuffed dog, to help with the expense of driving back and forth to treatments. He had grumbled earlier about having to drive two hours one way for chemo.

He looked at the stuffed dog and then held it up to his chin.

"Why are you doing this?" he asked. "I yelled at you, and even told you I hated your God."

I told him I was there because I understood pain. "I'm sorry people hurt you. Your journey matters, and if I helped you see that today, even for one minute, then I can go home happy."

He looked a little suspicious. "So, you're not going to preach to me, or make me pray with you?"

I shook my head. "I'm here to let you know you are loved. That's it."

In a hurting world, love transcends pain every time. It preaches louder than any sermon, and cuts through the fear and doubt.

I was about to stand up when he grabbed my hand and gave it a squeeze. "I'm sorry," he whispered. "And thank you." Tears had pooled in his eyes.

Years ago, as I sat in that same spot with mom during a tough chemo treatment, God knew that on another day, I would sit here again with someone who walked the same journey and needed hope. What we go through on our worst day can be used for a greater purpose later, when our journey is behind us.

As I left the center, clouds had formed on the horizon, and it was raining. I could smell spring in the air. The journey through the darkness of cancer and my own autoimmune disease has taught me to feel everything, even when it hurts. I didn't have an umbrella, but I didn't need one. I remembered the man's tears, the way love drowned his anger, and I lifted my head to feel every raindrop on my face.

Comfort Food

Grandma Mabel and the Seasons

It's October, and in this new season, I can smell the peanut brittle, divinity, and boiled custard. If you are familiar with boiled custard, then you know I'm remembering holiday baking. These are memories that are wrapped around Grandma Mabel, who would always begin preparing holiday goodies early, and often with me by her side. Grandma taught me to bake, and I'm sure she had to pray for extra patience when I showed up with my little apron and eager smile. I always liked the eating more than the baking!

I found Grandma's Bible today, and when I opened it to her favorite passage, a photo of her fell out. All the memories flooded back to me – how she loved the Lord with all her heart and loved her family in a way that made each one of us feel special. She knew what mattered in life, and she kept her priorities focused on what was eternal, not allowing the noise of life to sway her. The verse she loved gives me strength in this new season: *Now to him who is able to do immeasurably more than all we ask or imagine, according to his power that is at work within us* (Ephesians 3:20).

Seasons represent change, and that's not always comfortable. But it is necessary. The leaves are changing, and there are circumstances in our lives that will also change. People will leave, jobs will transition, some of us will be uprooted and replanted somewhere else. God has this season in His hands. Fear not, and don't take the season back. Allow the change to come and set your eyes on the Savior. He knows every change that is on the horizon, and He will walk with you through those changes.

After Grandma went to heaven, Mom used to long for just one more conversation with her. We all need the kind of wisdom that reminds us the best is yet to come. I give thanks every day that I had solid examples of women who focused on the mission, never compromised, and replaced the noise with the words of Jesus and the promises of scripture.

I smile when I remember those delicious kitchen smells, knowing that Mom and Grandma are together. Even though I miss them, it makes me happy to know these wise women are once again having conversations. If they were here, they would tell you to embrace the new season, welcome change, and trust that God has prepared something better than we can ever imagine.

Home Sweet Home

I walked in the door and the smell of comfort food enveloped me, a reminder that I was home. After two days of camp, I had called Mom and Dad and said those familiar words: "I want to come home!" I was the kid willing to endure the humiliation of walking from the camp cabin, my bag packed, knowing some kids were whispering "homesick" as they watched me leave. It didn't matter what anyone else thought because I knew the homesickness would disappear when I slid into the backseat. I walked into the house that day and smelled those home-cooked green beans, ham, and potatoes. The memory is vivid, and it reminds me home is a healing, comforting place. After a tough week, I made that same meal, and all the cares of the day lifted. I was home.

The past 18 months of pandemic have redefined the concept of home for so many people. For some, it represents joy, safety, and restoration, while for others, it brings feelings of pain, abandonment, and hopelessness. During this year of unknowns, we all feel like the ground is shaking beneath our feet. As one of my dear friends put it, "It feels like the fear is looming and the floor is about to fall out from underneath us." Many of us are grasping for a new normal, and desperate to leave behind all those unknowns. We want to slip into that backseat and head to a safe place where everything is predictable and steady.

I spent a day visiting a terminally ill friend and saying my goodbyes to her – as she says – "a see you later visit." After tears and the last heartbreaking farewell, I left with a familiar feeling of homesickness. It has been a month of losing dear friends and seeing others fight their way through tough battles. I sat at the stoplight on the way home and let the tears flow. "I want to go home from camp!" I said at one point. Oh, how I wished I could pick up the phone and ask Mom and Dad to rescue me from the uncertain and shaky ground beneath my feet. But as soon as the words were out of my mouth, I felt a calm assurance from the Lord that reminded me, *You are home.* He showed me, again, that home is not defined by the comforting meals, the safety of Mom and Dad's backseat, or even the actual dwelling. Home is His presence within my heart that brings me back to the safe place. It melts fear and anxious thoughts, quiets noise, and eases sadness. I only need to close my eyes, and I am home. The Lord is with me at all times and in every place I step, His arms are outstretched to welcome me back. I need the safety of His arms, especially during these uncertain days. The reality of this truth gives me a warm peace and a deep knowing that everything will be okay (Philippians 4:7).

Home and family are the vessel God chose when He ushered Jesus into a cold, dark world. God is preparing a forever home for me in heaven, but His Spirit lives inside me here on earth and I am never separated from His presence. Through the COVID pandemic, world turmoil and constant change, the presence of God is within me, and this is my home.

How lovely is your dwelling place, Lord Almighty! My soul yearns, even faints for the courts of the Lord; my heart and my flesh cry out for the living God. Even the sparrow has found a home, and the swallow a nest for herself, where she may have her young – a place near your altar, O Lord Almighty, my King and my God. Blessed are those who dwell in your house; they are ever praising you (Psalm 84:1-4).

This Psalm captures our longing for home, and acknowledges that the soul yearns to be in the place where God dwells. That, my friends, is our home, sweet home.

Clara's Pot Roast

When Clara entered a room, you knew she was there. Her raspy voice hurled out profanities and her rough-around-the-edges exterior was on full display. Clara was the cleaning lady at the apartment complex I managed years ago. Her life had been hard, and it showed on her face. The abuse she endured had taken a toll on her, and she put up a guard to keep anyone else from hurting her.

Everyone tried to steer clear of Clara, but I had a soft spot for her. Her husband left her and she was raising a teenage son on her own, but he was the light of her life. She was determined to be a good mother, and sometimes she would end up in my office for a conversation about raising kids. She often challenged me about my faith and questioned how anyone could believe in a Jesus they had never seen. Clara told me she would never be a Christian, since "those people" were fake, mean, and full of deceit.

I prayed for Clara every day and asked God to help me be the person who didn't give Christians a bad name. I knew the best way to show Clara a different view of Christians was simply to love her. But on certain days, she was a very hard person to love. Her pain was so evident, and she didn't want anyone getting too close.

One day, the phone rang in my office. The voice on the other end was a family member of Clara's, letting me know Clara's son had been killed in a car accident. He died instantly, and when I hung up the phone, I stared at the wall for what seemed like hours. I couldn't comprehend or process the terrible news. What words would I say to Clara? I went home and spent a restless night, praying and wondering what help to give at a time like this. At one point in the night, I asked (again) for God to give me direction. And in my heart, I clearly heard two words. *Pot roast.*

Really, God? I had never made pot roast, but I had a recipe from my grandmother. The more I thought about pot roast, the more sense it made. Comfort food. I got up the next morning and headed to the store where I bought the biggest roast I could find, and vegetables that would also go into the pot. My entire day focused on pot roast. I rolled up my sleeves and prayed over that roast before I started. Everything went into the pot and simmered until the meat fell apart. Just like my grandmother's.

I packed everything up and prayed for eloquent words as I approached Clara's porch. As soon as Clara opened the front door, I knew God wanted me to keep my mouth shut. No words would heal the pain, so I stood on the porch with my pot roast and waited for Clara to speak. She took the pan, set it on a table nearby, and grabbed me in a hug as she sobbed. This hardened woman cried from a deep part of her soul, and I felt those cries rise straight up to heaven. Jesus loved Clara, and I prayed my pot roast might plant a tiny seed that would begin a work in her life.

I looked over her shoulder as she held on to me and watched a family member dish out the pot roast onto paper plates. Clara's relatives looked exhausted and shocked. A pot roast seemed like a small thing considering the tragedy they were enduring.

Clara never came back to work after her son died, but one morning I was opening emails and came across one with the subject line, "Pot roast." It was from Clara, who no longer cleaned apartments, but now worked at a church, cooking meals for homebound people. I had to read her email twice for the news to sink in. Her specialty, and favorite dish to make was pot roast.

I thought my meal and wordless hug were insignificant, but Clara didn't think so.

"Lisa, you were the only one who came and brought food," Clara said. It had made an impact on her because the food and hugs didn't come with empty words, trite cliches, or preaching. "You were just there, and you loved us."

After Clara went to work at the church, she was eating a pot roast sandwich one day and decided to give God a try. She remembered a moment of wordless love. A small seed planted.

So many times, it isn't our words that lead others to God, but our silence. I love this quote: "Lighthouses don't fire cannons to call attention to their shining. They just shine." When I think about the times I have been moved the most, it's when I've witnessed someone living their life instead of shouting it. Living your words may begin with the smallest seed: a smile, a hug, holding a hand in the darkest moment. And a pot roast.

No words, just love lived out loud.

The Cake Fail

My first attempt at a gluten-free, sugar-free cake was in the oven, a masterpiece I put together in between appointments. I had been craving something sweet but needed to bake the cake quickly and move on with my day. When the timer went off, I raced to the oven. The cake looked like the masterpiece I envisioned, so I set in on the counter to cool.

My skills as a chef are lacking, but I love to bake and had recently begun a gluten-free journey, so it was time to sharpen those skills. I couldn't wait to dig in, and with my dog at my feet, I sliced a big piece. This was my first taste of anything sweet in two months, and I gave myself permission to indulge in two slices.

My enthusiasm came to a screeching halt as soon as I put the first bite in my mouth. It wasn't sweet and tasted nothing like a cake. What kind of crazy recipe was this? I retraced my steps and realized I had used chili powder instead of cinnamon. And the sugar substitute was still on the counter in the measuring cup, along with my reading glasses, which I had not worn while reading the spice labels. This is what happens when I hurry, which is something God and I are working on.

I threw the cake in the sink and called it a failure. My dog watched with what looked like sympathetic eyes, but I think she was just sad to see food going down the disposal.

While I washed the baking pan, I realized there might be a lesson in this disaster. I'm an impatient person and want God to hurry things along. I want immediate answers to health questions instead of waiting it out, trusting God to walk with me on whatever journey lies ahead. God has given me wonderful gifts in my life, and they are all in His hands. He is putting them together, measuring perfectly and working everything out in His timing. He knows what it takes for a perfect recipe, and how long the cake needs to bake. That means heat. So often refinement is what we need to move forward. Often, God works things out in those uncomfortable places, and what emerges is a wonderful masterpiece. He can bring healing and miracles, but first we must give Him time to bake the cake.

Thinking about life this way might seem a far reach, but I'm a visual person, and sometimes I need a picture. The cake analogy put things in a whole new perspective for me that day. I thought about Shadrack, Meshach and Abednego in that fiery furnace in Daniel Chapter 3. That story always humbles me but is also a reminder of what God can do when we trust that He holds our life in His hands. I can picture those three boys, scared, but certain they served a God who would deliver them. They took one step in, and God showed up. He always shows up, but He wants me to take that step. Trust that He knows the perfect timing, process, and the ingredients to add (and leave out). He creates the masterpiece.

I laughed at my dreadful cake. Chili powder? I don't want to taste it again, but I do want to remember the lesson God gave me. He can teach us even when we're in the middle of a mess. I didn't bake a cake again that day. Instead, I drove to Whole Foods for a fruit smoothie. There weren't any lessons in the smoothie, but it sure tasted better!

Cookies on the Table

The laughter in the café echoed, and I ignored it, focused on getting in and out with my juice. The laughter continued, and when I looked over at the table, I realized they were pointing and cackling at *me*. Was there something hanging out of my nose, or was my zipper open? I checked both possibilities, but nothing was amiss. What could be so funny? My first thought was to get in the car and go somewhere else, but I was already in line. I could feel my heart racing all the way up to my nostrils, my pulse pounding as I wondered what was wrong with me. Why were they pointing and laughing? I had walked in to get a juice, and now I was on display.

As I stood trying to figure it out, my mind went back to a conversation with one of my daughters about authenticity. Being real. Showing who we are and not caring what the world thinks. It's about what God thinks, we both agreed, and having the courage to take our masks off.

My daughter and I looked up the word *authenticity*, and this is what we found: loyalty, faithfulness, sincerity, devotion, honesty, steadfastness, fidelity, safety, security, reliable, firm, unimpeachable, real, not copied or duplicated. As I read those words, it makes me want to forget the masks. Those are some amazing attributes and I want all of them!

The enemy uses such trivial things to trip us up and make us lose sight of the authenticity God wants us to walk in. The enemy is always there with a counterfeit lie to confuse us. If you've ever listened to those lies, you know what I'm talking about: *You aren't pretty enough. You aren't smart enough. You aren't spiritual enough. You are not enough.* I've listened to those lies more times than I want to admit. There are days when I wake up and the sound is roaring in my ears like a hungry lion. But behind those roars, if I listen closely, I hear the still, small voice of the Holy Spirit reminding me who I am, and that I am enough.

As I stood in line, thinking about masks and authenticity, I decided that being authentic also means that we don't give in to fear. As soon as my juice was in hand, I bought some gluten-free cookies and decided I would go say hello to the table of laughing people. What did I have to fear? I walked over, my heart pounding, and set the cookies on the table in front of the laughing ladies. They looked delighted when I asked if they would like some cookies with their coffee. We began to talk, and they told me every few weeks they meet to share gluten-free recipes and support one another. Imagine their surprise at my offering. I shared my story of celiac disease, and told them I understood, since both my son and I have to eat gluten-free. In fact, I had just told a friend that I needed help learning how to be creative with gluten-free cooking. And piled on the table in front of me were a stack of recipes, and a group of women to help.

As it turns out, they weren't laughing at me at all, but telling each other funny stories, not realizing they were looking at me, or pointing my way. I had bought into the lie that I was a joke, which is so easy to do. God reminded me of that conversation with my daughter about authenticity.

We choose who we believe. God tells us we are enough. The enemy tells us we're a joke. Who will you trust? I'm taking my mask off and believing God when He reminds me I'm unique and created by His loving hand. I'm comforted knowing that God is dancing and singing at the very thought of me and you (Zephaniah 3:17).

That's enough to make me want to rip that mask off, show my true self, and love who I am.

Tin Box of Memories

I found the little tin box under old files, books, and dusty folders. It looked exactly like I remembered, and I held the box close, knowing what was inside: recipes on index cards in Mom and Grandma's handwriting, passed down through generations. I had been looking for the tin box for years, certain it was gone for good.

Each card held a memory. Grandma's pot roast with potatoes and carrots welcomed us every Sunday after church; egg sandwiches with the secret ingredient – bacon grease – were a Sunday evening staple as we sat around the television watching the Ed Sullivan show; Mom's homemade stew waited for us on the fireplace hearth after a cold bus ride home from school; the cookies Grandma made every year for my mom's piano recitals were a tradition. Ah, the cookies. Grandma baked and I snatched about half the batch as fast as she could pull them out of the oven. No one else's cookies tasted like hers. I remember her joy in the kitchen and conversations we shared as she baked and cooked.

But the precious jewel waiting for me in the box was the recipe for boiled custard. If you have eaten boiled custard, you know the warmth and love that goes into this dish. I can remember sitting around the table, sharing stories while we drank the custard. It was my dad's favorite, and he remembered enjoying buttery cornbread that accompanied the custard as he was growing up. It brought back comforting memories for both of us.

With Mom and Dad gone now, I thank God for giving us tangible keepsakes of the people we've lost. As I thumbed through, I came across Mom's chicken and noodles recipe, and remembered our conversation as she tried to teach me how to make the homemade noodles. I was young, and she was patient with my efforts. After we finished, Mom and I sat at the table while our dish cooked. We talked about recipes, and why they were so important, and then Mom gave me a lesson for my soul.

Life, she said, is like a recipe. You shouldn't rush the process, and make sure you put in the right ingredients. The measurements need to be correct, and it all begins with love. She referred to a spiritual recipe for a blessed life filled with abundance and miracles. Our personal relationship with Jesus sets the foundation for a wonderful recipe. Add goodness and a sprinkle of knowledge. Don't forget to add Godliness and some self-control (just be sure to measure those well). Mix everything together and bake with love, then serve with much prayer and thanksgiving. Each step and ingredient matter, she said, and our open heart and willingness to follow each step makes it a beautiful recipe every time.

I'm thankful my mom and dad gave not only the joy of comfort food, but the comfort of knowing life goes on after we leave this earth. As Mom battled cancer, she lost her ability to taste that delicious food, so she turned to the scriptures. We would read psalms together on those long chemo treatment days, when we were tired and needing a reminder God was pulling us through. Scripture promised us there were better days ahead. The Psalms has become my necessary book of the Bible for those times when I need soul comfort food. Reading the passages assures me God is our everlasting comfort.

After going through my newly found recipe box, I decided to try the recipe I loved most – the one that took patience and exact measurements. Boiled custard. As I mixed, stirred, and waited for it to boil, I thought about how God knows what we need in each season. He gently measures, mixes, and is aware of how much heat we can withstand. He reminds us throughout the process that we are loved and treasured. Some recipes are more complicated than others, but God always knows what He is doing.

My boiled custard tasted pretty good, almost exactly how I remembered it. It's not Grandma's, but it gives me something to work toward, and a lot of warm memories to cherish along the way.

Joy Jumps

Where Joy Lives

There is a photo from one of our recent Lisa Bain Ministries events that gives me a laugh every time. It's a stuffed version of an emoji that looks like a pile of poop. I know what you're thinking: *Who needs that?* Turns out, I do. For one reason, it's good for a humorous photo opportunity. And the other reason? I need to remember those "poopy" days, months, years. I've had a few, and you have too. You know the place: stuck on the smelly side of things, waiting for the fragrant aroma of joy to return.

There is a difference between happiness and joy. We use the words interchangeably, but they come from two different places. Happiness is based on a feeling that goes along with favorable circumstances. It's often short and fleeting. Joy, however, can exist and even flourish in difficult situations. It's dependent on God's spirit and is a fruit He produces.

But the question is always there. How can you walk in joy when tears block your vision? When I walked through one of the toughest seasons of my life recently, I had to mine deep for joy. I needed it to sustain me through the days when sadness was my constant companion. I discovered that connection with other people is a vital part of joy. Without that connection, communication fades and we feel hopeless. It's the same with our connection to God. It's difficult to feel connected to Him when my sadness keeps me at a distance. I will find excuses to stay in my negative place, and before I know it, joy has become a casualty. It's gone. Keeping my connection with God a priority keeps drawing me back to the joy.

Connecting with authentic people who will support and pray for us during our dark days is another key to walking in joy. In that photo with my favorite emoji, my friends are standing behind me, just like in life. Genuine friends plant their feet in place and cheer us on when we feel like we're left holding the stuffed poop emoji. God will reveal those genuine friends and provide us with an inner circle of people who keep us accountable. This discovery of a trustworthy inner circle has been a treasure for me, as they remind me to keep my focus on the mission, not the noise. They communicate and pray for me every day, laugh with me, and don't mind if I ugly cry in front of them. If you don't have these kinds of friendships, ask the Lord to put them in your path. You're going to need them along the way, and they will need you, too.

The Bible encourages us to *rejoice with those who rejoice* (Romans 12:15). Celebrating and rejoicing take the focus off ourselves and place it on others. Giving and helping others during the darkness pulls you out of your box and into the light – where joy lives!

On those dark days, I remind myself to "choose gratitude" instead of "choose joy." I find that when I embrace an attitude of praise and thanksgiving, the joy follows. When I was lying in a fetal position on my kitchen floor, broken and unable to move because of a betrayal, I asked my husband to put my favorite praise hymns and songs on repeat. My heart was so broken that at first, I only listened, soaking in the words. After a few hours, my lips moved as I quietly sang along, and the heaviness in my heart lifted. It was as if brokenness could not continue during praise. My vision cleared, and I could utter the words, "Thank you, Jesus, for this place I am in, because you are with me." His presence was the sustaining joy in that broken place.

Those tough blows and painful trials don't have to destroy our joy, even though they may leave us reeling and searching for answers. The joy is still present, and it will carry us through. The Apostle Paul wrote about his hardships and referred to being *sorrowful, yet always rejoicing* (2 Corinthians 6:10). In James, this theme appears again as we are encouraged to consider it pure joy when we face all kinds of trials, because there is the potential for a positive outcome.

When life is happy and sunny, I may have temporal blessings, but His presence is felt with deeper intensity in the struggle. In the moments when I choose joy amid the broken places and cry for help, He answers. When circumstances overwhelm me and my hope is slipping away, I cling to God, and then something extraordinary happens. He shows me His glory, and the glimpse of that glory overshadows my suffering. My focus is no longer on removing the trial; it shifts to knowing God deeper and experiencing more of Him.

Choosing joy is tough on certain dark, clouded days. But the torrential downpours in life that leave me feeling hopeless are where I find Jesus. His presence is more powerful than any broken place, His promises far greater than any negative circumstance.

Puddle Jumping

Macy looked like she was dressed for a party. Sundress. Sandals. Hair neatly brushed. But that was all about to change. She was holding her mother's hand as they walked down the street, and in an instant, she broke loose and headed for the puddle. Before her mother could stop Macy, she was stomping through the ripples of water, her white sundress now the color of mud, and her face and hair splattered with brown water. "Macy, NO!" her mother yelled, but it was too late. Macy was a mess and having the time of her life in that puddle.

I'm thinking about Macy and her expression of pure joy when she saw that puddle. In her eyes, it wasn't a hole filled with muddy water, but an opportunity that was made for fun! How do I look at the trials – puddles – that are in front of me? Some are muddier than others, and I can't always tell how deep one is until I stomp into it. Do I consider those as dangerous sinkholes that I work to avoid? Or do I look at them like Macy looked at that puddle, finding the delight even in the unpredictable muck and mud? God not only wants me to get through those trials, He wants me to find joy when I'm in the middle of them. He doesn't want me to go through a day when there is no fun and laughter, even when I'm knee deep in brown water. Life is full of puddles and sinkholes, but He doesn't want me to drown in them.

2020 was quite a year to put this to the test. Some might even say it was a sinkhole year, filled with challenges none of us could have imagined. Some days, I need a lifejacket just to get through it. How can we possibly find joy and laughter through trials? As soon as I ask that question, God reminds me to close my eyes, take a deep breath, and know that He's beside me and will hold me up through it all. I won't sink. I can enjoy the jump (or stomp!). What I see is what I am looking for, and if I see the insurmountable, then I will miss the joyful jump into the puddle. It's the difference between childlike faith and fear. If only we could face those puddles the same way Macy did.

On my morning run today, I jumped in every puddle on my route. It had rained earlier, so there were many in my path. God wants me to enjoy the journey, even if it might mean parts of it are messy and frightening. Changing my perspective reminds me He is beside me as I let go of the "sinkhole" mentality. There really can be joy in the muddy, unpredictable puddles ahead. So, get your rain boots on and let's jump!

The Jar

I sat staring at the jar, feeling anything but joy. Every day, I pull a slip of paper from my Joy Jar with a random act of kindness printed on it. The act is always something small, but the impact can be big. That day, I didn't want to reach into the jar. My body was not catching up to my brain, and I wanted to stay in bed.

"Just take one step outside of the box, Lisa, and ask God to take it from there." Mom's words were repeating in my head. "Even on the toughest days, there is always a way to serve and give back. Just take that first step." Those words had helped me through Mom's cancer battle and my autoimmune journey. Purpose. Serving. Trusting.

I made my Joy Jar to remind me that no matter what life throws my way, whether big or small, I can always turn it around and give back. How hard is it to make a phone call and let someone know you're praying for them? And how many times have I met people with amazing stories and miracles? Plenty. And today would be no different.

I took that first step and pulled from the jar. The paper said, "Mail an encouraging letter to someone in need of a smile." I instantly knew who needed this letter, so I took out pen and paper and wrote words of encouragement. I sealed the envelope and Mabel Joy and I headed to the post office to drop it in the mail slot. But as we began our journey, there was construction at every turn, and we were getting nowhere fast. A route that should have taken five minutes stretched into twenty, and my patience was running out. I wished that Joy Jar had given me something different, and I was about to grumble when I remembered what I prayed that morning as my feet hit the floor.

Lord, may every step and minute of this day be directed by you.

I often forget that prayer when the detours take me to unplanned places. My own agenda gets in the way of the paths God wants to take me on. I breathed deeply and remembered that God always directs my steps. He always has a plan.

We finally made it to the post office, and after mailing my letter, I headed to the next stop on my list of errands. I was pulling away from the post office when I saw an elderly woman with a letter in her hand, struggling to make it to the door. She was walking with a cane, and something in my spirit shouted at me to help her. I pulled back into the parking lot and jumped out quickly. I had just come up behind the woman when her cane missed a step and she stumbled backwards into my arms. If I had hesitated for a second, I wouldn't have caught her. The timing was God's, and He gave me the strength to do what needed to be done. I helped her stand back up, grabbed her cane, and told her we would walk to the mailbox together. After she dropped her letter in the box, we turned toward her car. She was shaking. "Thank you, thank you," she repeated. I learned her name is Mary, and she was recently widowed and trying to make it on her own. She had been fighting her own health battle, and in the middle of it, lost family members to COVID. Her path of loneliness was scary, but she was doing her best. Her husband used to take care of the mail runs, she told me, but now it was her job.

Mary and I had an instant connection, and I thanked her for sharing her story with me. There was an extra Resilience Care Box in my car, so I gave it to her. She opened the box, then buried her face in her hands, crying so hard she couldn't speak. I let Mabel out of the car so she could snuggle with Mary for a moment. As Mabel leaned in, my new friend's arms reached around her furry neck for a comforting snuggle. Then Mary turned to me and held out her arms for a hug, thanking me again. "You lifted me up in every way possible today. You were an answer to my prayer."

I think she had it backwards. Mary was an answer to *my* prayer, and it began with my Joy Jar. The construction delay felt like a useless detour, but it allowed me to be there for Mary at the moment she needed me. It was God's perfect timing for both of us. That day, I had felt frustrated and unprepared for the unexpected. I wanted to stay in my comfortable place and skip the Joy Jar. But God caught me, reminding me of Mom's words and calming my spirit. He gave me His strength so I could catch someone else in need. That simple act of kindness changed everything about my day. And I have a new friend.

What is in your Joy Jar? Take that first step and see where God leads. He wants to accompany you on a journey where small acts can have a big impact. Lives will be changed, and one of those will be yours.

Jumping Off Cliffs

I posted on Facebook about jumping out of my comfort zone in a big way, which prompted a friend to ask if I was going to another country. She thought that moving away from what is comfortable and toward the unknown must mean mission work across the ocean. But sometimes, God takes us on a mission trip right where we are. I'm staying here, I explained to her, and yet, I'm not staying in the same place I've been. Confusing, I know.

I picture a sharp cliff, with sparkling blue water beneath it, and I'm at the top, my toes at the edge and my arms outstretched. I'm a little afraid, and I have a lot of questions about how this is going to work. But God says, "Trust me with everything. I'm here waiting." And then, in my mind, I see myself jumping off with no life raft beneath, only the faith that God will catch me. The first step is the scariest – when we move out of our comfort zone and the safe ground we've been standing on. But every time, He is there to catch me and take me to unimaginable places. And He carries me to safe ground. When I picture this kind of faith, I wonder if I really believe He will catch me. Do I have the faith to take the first step? Some days I'm ready to run straight off the cliff, and other days I'm crawling on the ground away from it. But God whispers to me, "Fear not."

In Jeremiah, God tells us to call to Him, and He will answer and show us great and unsearchable things we do not know. Not only will He catch us as we take those leaps of faith, but He will give us the answers we need to take the next step.

I'm realizing this cliff jumping is true for so many. Precious friends are going through trials, and they have questions none of us can answer. Some things just don't make sense. And yet, jumping off the cliff means we trust God has reasons, even when the answers don't come. God takes me beyond the answers to a place of trust, rest, and joy.

Mom and I talked once about taking those leaps, and what happens when in the middle of jumping off the cliff, we start to doubt. We have questions. And we wonder if God is going to be there to catch us at the bottom. She looked at me and said, "Lisa, I don't understand so many things in life, but I hang on to this." And she began to sing one of her favorite hymns, *We'll Talk It Over*. The song talks about deep shadows that cause our heart to fear, and how someday, we'll talk with God about all the "whys." But for now, we can walk in peace and allow Him to lead, saving our questions for another day.

Tears were in her eyes as she sang, and it was as if she had jumped off a cliff and was resting in His arms. Mom's journey had brought her to that cliff many times over the past year, looking down at the deep waters, and facing the unknown. It was frightening, and she didn't have answers, but she knew she was safe with Jesus. Her life was a living testimony to the kind of faith that takes us far from our comfort zone.

Am I taking a mission trip? Yes! But not the kind that involves a plane ticket or packing a bag. I'm stepping out of comfortable places and jumping off that high cliff. I'm trusting God with the things I don't understand, the trials and hurdles that seem insurmountable, all the questions that are unanswerable.

Someday, we'll have the answers. I'll ask the reasons and He'll tell me why. But until then, I'm trusting in the One whose arms are outstretched to catch me. There is joy at the end of the jump, and a peace that only comes from resting in the promises of my Savior.

Yes Lord, Even in a Chicken Suit

On days when it's hard to smile, I reach into my closet and bring out the chicken suit. I realize the last sentence makes me sound like a crazy woman, but my chicken suit has led to some amazing miracles. Do I look ridiculous when I wear it? Yes, but God has used it to bless so many people, including me.

A dear friend and I met for coffee one day, and her tears flowed as she told me about her job loss and the stress she felt. We prayed together, but I wanted to do more. I silently asked God to show me how to help in a tangible way. God heard, and at that moment, He began to answer both our prayers. As I drove home, I felt God asking, "Are you willing, Lisa?" I think He was smiling. Of course I was willing! "Anything, Lord. Anything."

A few days later, a friend called to tell me she had been laughing all morning at a photo of me on Facebook wearing my chicken suit in my backyard. "There's no way you would ever wear that thing out, is there?"

"Most definitely," I told her, and she took me up on the challenge.

"I'll give you $100 if you wear your chicken suit to Starbucks for coffee."

"You already know I will do this, so why are you going to pay me?" I asked.

Her reply: "Lisa, sometimes God works in mysterious ways."

Once again, I pointed out that she didn't have to pay me since I was more than willing to wear my crazy chicken suit to Starbucks. In the middle of a sentence, I remembered I had asked God to give me a tangible way to help my friend. And here it was. I could give that $100 to help after her job loss. I stopped protesting and agreed to wear the suit and take the money.

Wearing my chicken suit to Starbucks (and yes, I drank coffee in it), opened the door to helping my friend. Then, another friend asked if I would consider visiting a nursing home or hospital with my therapy dog while wearing my chicken suit. That was a no-brainer. God opened doors left and right, as only He can. It was amazing and hilarious – the chicken lady and the service dog. God is creative, and He knows what will bring smiles to faces, and joy to hearts.

Over the years, God has provided funds for me to give to others, but also opportunities to show up, which is often just as important. And many times, I showed up wearing my chicken suit because I've learned never to put God in a box or expect that He will allow me to stay in one. He's always one step ahead, surpassing the limitations I put on myself. All this time, I had a chicken suit in my closet that was meant to bless others. Yes, God uses anything and everything to fulfill His purposes.

Months later, my service dog, Holly, and I visited a nursing home, which had become a regular thing for us. I wore my chicken suit, and was tempted to ask myself, "Why am I doing this in a chicken suit, looking like a crazy woman?" But I was exactly where I was supposed to be, and I knew this with certainty when a resident came up to me, her eyes sparkling.

"I sure do love you, Chicken Lady." She leaned over and kissed my cheek, and Holly got a kiss, too. My heart was full, and I knew God had a big purpose for my chicken suit. The Chicken Lady has shown up at many places since then, and every time, I remember how this journey started. A prayer. A phone call. And God, knowing that a service dog and a lady in a chicken suit bring the healing joy many people need.

Whether you are the one in need, or the person who wants to help, I challenge you to ask God for provision. He will bring what you need in ways you never dreamed, with joy along the path. Take it from the Chicken Lady with the service dogs. Giving and receiving in ways you never imagined is a journey that will change your life.

Shall We Dance?

Eight weeks after surgery, my doctor gave me the thumbs up to run again. My running shoes beckoned me toward my familiar route, and as I tied my shoelaces, my adrenaline was pumping. Running is excellent therapy, and I had missed it. The weeks I could not run gave me a new outlook on my feet and legs. I felt grateful that my body was ready and able to hit the pavement running.

I did a little victory dance as I started my run. The sun seemed to shine brighter, and the air was fresh. I lifted my arms, skipped, took a few turns, and did some fancy steps along the way. As I passed one driveway, I heard my little neighbor friend, Carly, ask, "Mommy, what's wrong with that lady?" My neighbor looked up at me and waved. "That's just Lisa. She does happy dances." I slowed my pace to listen to their conversation and heard Carly ask if she could also do a happy dance. By this time, I was close enough to talk to them, and I told Carly's mother that I would love for her to join me. Carly ran to me and we danced. And danced. A few people passing by stared in surprise. Another neighbor, an older man with a cane, joined in, and a few other neighbors who were out for a morning walk added their own moves. Our little gathering of street dancers was laughing and swaying to different rhythms, which made the dance more wonderful.

I waved goodbye after a few minutes and continued my run, feeling the energy of the impromptu party. I thought about each person who joined in. One neighbor was a caregiver for her terminally ill husband. Another had just said goodbye to her son, who was headed to Iraq. One neighbor wore a prosthesis and was dancing his own style. A lady who joined us had lost her mother recently, and another neighbor was recovering from a heart attack and battling depression. I knew each person and the hurdles they faced. Their challenges and uncertainties made mine seem small.

When I got home, there was a message on my phone from the neighbor who was caregiving for her husband. She thanked me for the street dance and said she got a glimpse of how we need to celebrate in dark times and remember to thank God for the little things in life. I agreed. It might be just a short dance, but it makes a big statement. We are shouting into the darkness that we will not allow it to defeat our joy. My neighbor and I talked about these hurdles we are all facing, and by the time we finished our conversation, we were both crying. We ended with a prayer.

I hung up the phone, amazed. Look what one dance can do! I asked myself if I notice those opportunities to dance in the dark times. It was a summer with so many hurdles put in front of our family. Cancer. Surgeries. Saying goodbye to my sister who moved to Canada. I wouldn't trade the hurdles, though. They bring lessons, and the opportunity to dance in the middle of the darkness.

I may not win any competition for flying over the hurdles, but I can dance my way through them. Life is not only about the journey, but how we choose to travel. Jesus gives us the dance, and the grace to hurdle over loneliness, pain, rejection, grief, anger, low self-esteem. God has a way over the hurdles, and He delights in surprising us. If my dance is imperfect or if I fall flat on my face, He catches me, and we finish the race.

There are days when I have a dance in my step, and days when I trudge along, tempted to give up, sit down, and throw myself a pity party. But the only way forward is to put one foot in front of the other and cry out to Jesus for help. He takes it from there. Before long, putting one foot in front of the other becomes a dance step. Whether it's a dance from the soul or a physical dance, our job is to let go and let God. We can't do it alone, but we have a God who leads us in the steps that bring lasting peace on the journey. Shall we dance?

Party Hats

I noticed the elderly man sitting alone on a bench, his hands covering his face. I had finished making hospital visits and delivering care boxes and was enjoying the mild summer breeze as I walked to my car. He heard me coming closer and lifted his head, giving me a faint smile.

"Hello ma'am. Isn't this weather nice?"

"It sure is," I replied. "I hope you're enjoying it too."

That quick exchange about the weather was all it took to begin a conversation. The man told me his wife had been gravely ill, and now he was losing her. There was nothing more the doctors could do, so she was on her way to hospice. He was taking a break to sit outside where he could breathe deeply, pray, and try to wrap his head around the news.

He seemed eager to talk about his wife, and his eyes sparkled as he spoke. She was the life of the party, full of joy and always passing it on to others. She gave constant encouragement and inspiration to everyone around her. He had married the love of his life 70 years ago, and the two of them had filled those years with such beautiful memories.

"Oh, she loved Jesus. Boy, did she love Jesus!" His eyes twinkled and then a moment of sweet laughter. "And now she gets to meet Him." That laughter was from a deep place in his soul, and I knew I wouldn't forget it. Even in his broken place that day, he could still find joy. He knew she wouldn't be with him on this earth much longer, but he wanted her to know she was being celebrated as she made her journey home.

"I don't want her homegoing to be sad," he said. "I want it to be a party. She loved parties." He paused for a moment before asking, "Does that sound weird?"

Obviously, he didn't know my history with chicken suits and party hats, so I told him about my mom, the hats, those funny dogs. And that chicken suit. We sat on the bench and laughed until our bellies ached.

I know it wasn't an accident that I met this precious man on the day I was delivering Resilience Care Boxes that contained, of course, party hats. We pack those hats in our boxes to symbolize choosing joy and celebration, even when we are walking through brokenness. I happened to have an extra care box, which was also not an accident. I retrieved the box from my car and brought it to my new friend.

"What's this?" he asked when I handed it to him.

I told him it was a gift of encouragement and hope as he walked through this last part of the journey with his sweet wife. "I'll be praying for you," I said.

He opened the box and the image of what happened next is something I'll always carry with me. He saw the party hat and grabbed it out of the box, clutching it to his heart as he cried. Tears were falling faster than he could wipe them. As they fell, he began to laugh, and the joy he felt at that moment radiated. I gave him a big hug, silently thanking God for my new friend.

He took a deep breath. "Okay, I'm ready. It's party time." My friend stood up and walked back to the hospital to be with his wife, clutching his box as if it were a treasure, and wearing that big party hat. I'll never forget the sight. The smile on his face told the story of how we can find laughter in the darkest places. It's always possible.

I think you know the rest of the story. It ended with me sobbing all the way to my car.

Divine appointments are just that. Divine. This moment was a gift not only for my new friend, but for me as well. I needed it, and I'll never forget it. My divine appointment confirmed once again all that I learned during my mom's cancer journey. I thought back to the conversations we had about party hats, and how it's possible to find laughter even in the most broken places. But we must look for it. I was reminded of her funeral, filled with people wearing party hats, and then I thought about what a party it must have been at the moment she met her Savior. My new friend's wife will soon meet my mom, and knowing Mom, she'll be wearing a party hat.

The encounter that day would not have happened if not for the legacy Mom left. Those Resilience Care Boxes would not have been in my car, and a chicken suit and party hat would not have been in my story. Lisa Bain Ministries would not have become a reality without her legacy. God knew on that first day Mom and I wore our party hats to chemotherapy that I would someday sit on a bench with a grieving man who also needed a party hat.

Life is short. Choose to celebrate every second. Find beauty in the broken – it's there if you look for it. And have a party hat by your side! You never know when you'll need it.

About the Author

 Lisa Bain is the founder of Lisa Bain Ministries, a nonprofit organization that delivers hope and support to those who are facing illness, a special need, or a crisis. She is the author of three previous books, Joy in the Journey: Finding Laughter and Miracles in Very Dark Places, Life Outside the Box, and It's Better Out Here. Lisa and her husband Skipper live in Tulsa and have four children and two grandsons. You can find her at lisabain.com, where she writes regularly on her blog.

Made in the USA
Columbia, SC
16 October 2022